PARTNERS
IN ENTERPRISE
The Worker Ownership Phenomenon

To the memory of my father, Morris Quarter.

J.Q.

To my hard-working parents.

G.M.

PARTNERS
IN ENTERPRISE
The Worker Ownership Phenomenon

**BLACK
ROSE
BOOKS**

Montréal - New York

edited by
Jack Quarter and George Melnyk

Black Rose Books No. R 135

Hardcover ISBN: 0-921689-45-4
Paperback ISBN: 0-921689-44-6

Canadian Cataloguing in Publication Data
Main entry under title:

Partners in enterprise

Includes bibliographical references.
ISBN 0-921689-45-4 (bound) -
ISBN 0-921689-44-6 (pbk.)

    1. Employee ownership--Canada--Case studies.
I. Quarter, Jack, 1941-   . II. Melnyk, George

HD5660.C2P37 1989   334'.6'0971   C89-090248-8

Cover design: Zèbre Communications Inc.

Black Rose Books

3981 boul. St-Laurent, #444
Montréal, Québec H2W 1Y5
Canada

340 Nagel Drive
Cheektowaga, N.Y. 14225
USA

Printed and Bound in Québec, Canada

Contents

List of Figures and Tables

Preface

It is quite common for Western countries such as Canada to be referred to as democracies. Compared to many other countries in the world where citizens are denied the right to elect their political representatives and are denied such basic civil liberties as open criticism of government and organizing in opposition to government policies, the Canadian experience is positive and progressive. Yet the reference to Canada as a democracy disguises the fact that there has been a lengthy process leading to our current accomplishments. It was not so long ago that women and people without property were denied basic sufferage. Nor is the process complete. Although there has been much progress in bringing democracy to political life, there are still other important facets of our society where the popular will is inconsequential to decisions that are taken.

Work is one such area. The vast majority of workers in the Western democracies lack even the most elementary voice in decisions that affect the business that employs them. In part, this is because they are not owners but employees who are hired by management representing owners.

This book is about a form of business -- the worker co-operative -- in which workers are owners. As owners-in-common, the workers elect the board of directors (usually from their group) and often demand a direct voice in enacting major policies. As such, the worker co-operative brings democractic practice to the workplace.

The essays in this book provide a record of the worker co-operative movement both as it stands at present and historically from the first experiments in the 1860s. They not only focus on the Canadian experience but also draw heavily on international examples. The essays discuss the many problems of development and note the significant accomplishments of the past decade.

The people who have contributed to this book are tied in with the movement, a movement that is evolving both in this country and internationally. Inevitably their views reflect the discussions and analyses that are occurring.

We dedicate this book to the many pioneers of the worker co-op. Their courageous efforts in demonstrating that democracy can function within the workplace will inspire others to take up the cause.

We also want to thank three people in particular who have assisted greatly with the preparation of this manuscript: Jo-Ann Hannah, who by far exceeded the call of duty in the editorial preparation; Rikki Hortian, who computed the copy under much time pressure and always with pleasantness; and Judith Brown who carefully read and re-read the manuscript.

We hope that this book accurately represents the accomplishments to date in the process of building democractic workplaces. We also hope that this book will move others to realize that they have a right to voice and vote in the decisions affecting their work.

Jack Quarter and George Melynk

Chapter 1

Worker Ownership: One Movement or Many?

Jack Quarter

"Workers of Canada unite to buy out their own companies." The unlikely source of that headline is *Small Business*[1], an advocacy publication for the small-business community. The accompanying story describes the purchase of several corporate divisions by small groups of employees, including their management. For example, Control Data, a computer software company with a head office in Mississauga, was purchased by 10 employees. There were 130 employees not included in the ownership group. Two months later, *Small Business* ran a feature about Lamford Forest Products near Vancouver.[2] Over 250 workers participated in the buyout of Sooke Forest Products, and each worker holds one voting share and has a similar financial stake.

These diverse examples reflect the problem of analyzing the muddy terrain known as worker ownership. Lamford Forest Products and Control Data are both labeled as "worker ownership," but are they part of the same movement? Do they share similar goals and aspirations? Worker ownership fails to conform to neat groupings. There are many different variations -- almost as many variations as there are worker-owned firms.

Worker Capitalism

Even though there is a broad range of worker-ownership models, a critical dimension for analyzing them is "corporate control." In the vast majority of companies with employee ownership, the workers lack corporate control. Workers remain employees, hired by the majority owners and taking direction from senior management who are beholden to the principal shareholders. Shares held by the workers may not entitle them to voting rights, and when they do, most often there is not a controlling interest. As such, this arrangement is often referred to either as "employee ownership" or as "employee share-ownership." It is a form of capitalism in which workers share more directly in the financial risks of the company that employs them. Economists Keith Bradley and Alan Gelb describe this change in corporate structure as "worker capitalism."[3]

The movement for employee share-ownership already is widespread in Canada. A 1986 survey by the Toronto Stock Exchange (TSE)[4] indicates that 63.3 per cent of companies listed on the Exchange had some form of employee share-ownership plan, and many companies offer their employees more than one type. The TSE survey also indicates that nearly one-third of the corporations have share-ownership plans which are open to all employees (not just officers, directors and senior management), and corporations normally provide financial assistance for employee purchases.

It is apparent that the corporate community is a primary force behind employee share-ownership. Sociologically, this movement is located within the corporate strata because it is believed that "employee share-ownership plans are having a direct and positive impact on productivity at Canadian corporations . . . ."[5] Employers also *perceive* a positive impact on "profitability" and "employee satisfaction." I emphasize "perceive" because it is perception rather than hard evidence which is fueling this movement. That's not to say that the perception is without foundation. There is evidence that employee ownership has benefits for corporations; but · this research, like research in general, has a lot of qualifiers, and the evidence is not totally conclusive.

In a careful review of this research, Richard Long, a professor of organizational behavior at the University of Alberta, concludes:

> Employee-owned firms clearly possess the potential for highly successful performance under appropriate circumstances.[6]

The "appropriate circumstances" that Long describes include a substantial, broadly-distributed employee stake in combination with effective participation in decision-making.

Other researchers underline the importance of participatory decision-making for successful employee share-ownership plans. For example, an American study by the General Accounting Office finds that employee share-ownership has no effect on corporate performance unless it is combined with a plan to increase employee participation in decision-making.[7] Indeed, it is not clear from that study whether positive benefits result from the combined effects of employee share-ownership and employee participation or whether employee participation alone is affecting corporate performance.

If the evidence from formal research is applied to corporations in the TSE study, few would meet the decision-making criteria deemed to be causing an improvement in corporate performance. Nevertheless, the TSE report recommends that "employers *should* [emphasis added] not only encourage widespread participation by employees, but should also assist employees in making larger annual contributions, and to retain such contributions, if possible, within their employee share-ownership plan."[8]

Retaining shares within the corporation, of course, increases the employees' financial dependence upon the company's performance. This dependence is made even more explicit when employees' shares are linked to profit or some other measure of company gain. When the link is to profit, the strategy is referred to as profit-sharing; when the link is to some other form of corporate performance (e.g., productivity), this strategy is referred to as gain sharing. There are many variations, a common feature of which is the link between employee shares and corporate performance.

Frank Stronach, chairperson of Magna International, a leading supplier of car parts to the American auto industry, is an advocate of this approach in Canada.[9] At Magna, 10 per cent of the company's annual pre-tax earnings go to employees. Stronach refers to this practice as "Fair Enterprise" because he believes it motivates the employees and checks corporate greed. He credits this approach with increasing company sales from $226 million in 1982 to $1 billion in 1987. It is also noteworthy that Magna's salaries are lower than those in unionized companies in the same industry and the workers do not have a pension fund.

Canadian Tire, a major retailer of auto and household accessories, is also a leading advocate of employee share-ownership.[10] Employees hold 12.5 per cent of the stock through a trust fund. This stake, which can be substantial for long-time employees, is a substitute for a company pension plan.

Encouraging wage restraint is another reason why large corporations turn to employee share-ownership. The TSE report notes that: "The majority of employers, 73 per cent, view employee share-ownership plans as having had no impact at all on wage restraint," but it goes on to say that "one of the most interesting aspects of the survey...was the finding that more than half of employees would accept wage concessions in exchange for shares if their companies were experiencing serious financial difficulties."[11]

Unionized employees were least positive about this trade-off; generally speaking, employee share-ownership has not been an important feature of organized labour's agenda in Canada. Support has been strongest when employee shares are a bonus rather than a substitute for acceptable salaries and benefits. When the Ontario government originally presented a proposal to give employees a small grant to purchase shares in their place of work, the Ontario Federation of Labour (OFL) lobbied against it. Former OFL president, Cliff Pilkey, referred to the proposal as a "joke."[12]

Interestingly, the Canadian Federation of Independent Business (an organization representing very small businesses) also opposed the plan. "With 85 per cent of Ontario firms employing fewer than 10 workers, the government's not serious about helping small business raise capital," said Judith Andrew, Director of Provincial Affairs at the Canadian Federation of Independent Business.[13]

Andrew's statement comes directly to the point, because the basis for supporting employee share-ownership is pragmatic: namely, the financial benefits to business. By contrast, most businesses do perceive the benefit because the plans are practical to set up and because they are seen as improving the corporation's competitive position. In the end, the provincial government was persuaded by the corporate sector and the grant was approved.

The American Movement

The American movement has been stimulated by a series of tax amendments in 1974 and in 1986 which led to the creation of employee stock-ownership plans (ESOPs). These are a type of employee-benefit plan through which a company either makes tax-deductible contributions of new issues of its stock to a trust fund for the employees or it uses cash to buy existing shares. Alternatively, the ESOP can be used to borrow money to buy shares. A 1985 study by the National Center for Employee Ownership, an advocacy group for ESOPs, estimates that the typical employee in an ESOP accumulates $31,000 (U.S.) over 10 years.[14] The company benefits because proceeds of the sale to the employees' trust are tax-deductible, thereby providing a cheap source of financing. Banks also are given a tax incentive to make loans to ESOPs at reduced rates because the interest on such loans is tax-deductible.

There is no similar tax arrangement in Canada. As of 1988, four provinces -- Alberta, Québec, British Columbia and Ontario -- provide either tax credits or grants to employees who purchase shares in their place of work. These arrangements encourage a nominal equity stake in the corporation, which is the typical pattern in Canada.

Although American corporations also have employee-share plans, the tax changes enacted in 1974 have led to more substantial forms of employee ownership. The 1986 alterations to the 1974 tax amendments require that the employees own at least 30 per cent of the equity in a closely-held company in order for the ESOP to qualify for tax write-offs.[15]

According to the National Center for Employee Ownership

nearly 9 million American employees were enrolled in 8,700 ESOPs by year-end 1987.[16] Employee stock-ownership plans are not being established on the fringe of the American economy.[17] They have been created in very large corporations such as AVIS,[18] and throughout the steel, transportation, food, and health-service industries. It is estimated that the United States government is losing about $2-3 billion per year in tax revenues because of ESOPs.[19]

In some ESOPs (usually corporations in financial difficulty), employees purchase the stock in the ESOP by wage deductions.[20] When this occurs, employees are given an equity stake in exchange for reduced wages. This arrangement provides a source of financing for the corporation and lowers labour costs, thereby making the corporation more competitive. The American labour movement has tended to accept this arrangement in industries which are under competitive pressure from other countries with lower wages. Recognizing the realities of his industry, United Steelworkers of America president, Lynn Williams, states:

> We did not form and develop our union for the purpose of becoming the owners of the mines, mills, factories, and foundries where our members work. However, I do not believe there is any practical or philosophical reason why unions and worker-ownership cannot co-exist . . . .

> In the metals' industries, the involvement of our union in employee stock-ownership plans has been a matter of necessity. In a number of cases, we have been approached by companies whose long-term viability was threatened by depressed conditions in the industry. In such cases, we have been willing to recommend, and have gained the approval of our members, for programs of wage and benefit investments under an employee stock-ownership plan. In essence, we have agreed to increase the employer's cash-flow and earnings by substituting an employee stock-ownership plan for some portion of wages and benefits which would otherwise be paid in cash.[21]

In most ESOPs, employees hold only a minority of the corporation's stock. There is an increasing number of ESOPs (almost 700 in 1987) in which employees have a majority or all of the stock.[22] Frequently, these corporations are no longer of interest to their previous owners, and employees purchase the company as an alternative to losing their jobs.

Even majority employee-equity in an ESOP does not necessitate employee control. The trustees may be bankers, community leaders, and businesspersons who are appointed when the ESOP is created. The 8,000-worker Weirton Steel plant in West Virginia is totally owned by its workforce (with unequal shareholdings), but the workers still do not elect the trustees of the ESOP, even though the company has been very profitable since the buyout.[23]

Although ESOPs have been criticized for not providing for employee control, these trusts were not established for that purpose. The ESOP was inspired by a book, *The Capitalist Manifesto*,[24] by investment-banker Louis Kelso and was advocated in the U.S. congress by former Louisiana Senator, Russell Long. The philosophy behind the trust is to strengthen capitalism by giving employees equity in their place of work. In one of his many speeches in favour of ESOP tax legislation, Long states:

It is difficult for me to believe that any thoughtful policymaker can think for a moment that socialism or communism is really in the best interests of his people . . . .

Yet if they look to us for leadership, what do they see? They see a nation in which 50 per cent of the privately-held capital is owned by only one-half of 1 per cent of the population . . . .

In fact, the ownership of productive assets in the United States -- in relative terms -- is about the same today as when Herbert Hoover succeeded Calvin Coolidge . . . .

We desperately need a working model of what we would advocate for other nations. And I firmly believe that employee stock-ownership is just such a model . . . .

What could be a better answer to the unfulfilled promises of communism?

We should also be asking how many people own something and how many don't? And how much do they own? Because if we haven't improved much on what it was fifty years ago, what is the matter with us? . . .

We have the opportunity to offer this nation as a model for others . . . .

What we must do is to save this world from something it definitely does not need by providing it with something it does need. And employee stock-ownership is a good place to start.[25]

Recently, ESOPs have been subject to much criticism in the American congress, in part over increasing tax write-offs and in part over the lack of workers' control. Chairperson of the Senate Labour Committee, Edward Kennedy of Massachusetts, has tabled legislation that would require full voting rights for employees in ESOPs owning more than 20 per cent of the shares in a company.[26] In defending ESOPs against their critics, Corey Rosen, director of the National Center for Employee Ownership, argues that they are primarily a "financing arrangement" not a form of workers' control.[27] Rosen states:

> About half of all ESOPs are used to buy the shares of a retiring owner. The sale usually takes place over several years. Should the owner be forced to give up control once the ESOP owns 51 per cent of the shares, few owners would sell to an ESOP, and would choose instead to sell to competitors or liquidators.[28]

Some ESOPs already have full voting rights for workers; indeed, some function on the co-operative principle of one worker/one vote (e.g., O&O supermarkets in Philadelphia).[29] However, the Kennedy legislation makes voting rights a requirement not an option. Michael Keeting, an ESOP lobbyist, has already indicated that there will be stiff opposition from the corporate community. Mandatory voting rights, he warns, could result in "nobody wanting to use them anymore."[30]

The Kennedy proposal reflects the American tradition for taking reform one step at a time. There still are many steps between trust funds that provide minority employee-ownership without voting rights (the norm for ESOPs) and corporations that are totally owned and democratically controlled by their workers (currently the exception). It is uncertain whether these many steps will ever be taken. In the interim, the ESOP must be seen for what it is -- a mechanism through which conventional corporations finance themselves by transferring equity without control to their workers.

The Canadian Scene

The employee-ownership movement in Canada has borrowed the American acronym, ESOP, though not the tax features. The Canadian plans usually involve the company providing financial assistance and the government providing tax credits for employees to purchase shares -- normally a nominal number. As in the United States, transferring corporate control to the employees is not part of this agenda. If employee shareholdings are substantial, they are often held in a trust controlled by management-appointed trustees.

The issue of corporate control arises most clearly where the employee stake is large. This circumstance usually occurs following a plant shutdown -- often plants with faltering reputations and badly in need of modernization (see Chapter 3 for a discussion of worker buyouts).

In view of the large number of plant shutdowns and corporate divestitures, there have been surprisingly few buyouts with broad and majority employee-ownership. Where broadly-based employee buyouts do occur, the arrangements are usually complex, and quite often a senior management group has the controlling interest, that is, the majority of voting shares (e.g., the Tembec paper mill buyout[31] in Temiskaming, Québec, or The Beef Terminal[32] in Toronto). Nevertheless, employees -- by virtue of their shareholdings -- do have voting rights and the opportunity to elect representatives to the board of directors.

Although usually falling short of corporate control, in employee-owned companies workers can have significant influence. Moreover, it is increasingly recognized in the conventional business community that employee shares without voting rights are unjust and can create false expectations that weaken morale. This issue came to the fore in the proposed sale of Canadian Tire Corporation by the Biles family, children of the founder. In a controversial decision, the TSE ruled that the employees had to be given the opportunity to convert their shares into common, voting stock and thereby participate in the decision about a proposed sale.[33]

Going beyond this particular ruling, the TSE also took an advocacy stance on employee voting rights. Its recent report on the topic states "that the most successful plans allocate voting rights to employee shareholders."[34] The rationale for this position is pragmatic and consistent with the total thrust of improving corporate performance:

> Employees were almost equally concerned that their ESOPs
> have given them no effective control over the decision-making
> process as they were about the value of their shares.
>
> This finding may reflect employees' disappointment at the
> implicit or explicit promises of management that employee
> share-ownership would bring employees greater influence
> within the corporate structure. It also seems possible that
> employees themselves are unaware of the rights and powers of
> minority shareholders.[35]

While pushing the idea of employees having "greater influence within the corporate structure," the TSE report is weak on specifics. The report's recommendations, though, are based on the conviction that increasing workers' influence upon decision-making will improve corporate performance. This same viewpoint has been promoted through another initiative referred to either as Quality of Working Life (QWL)[36] or socio-technical design.[37] Canadian corporations are introducing QWL programs, but with a small number of exceptions, these programs are cosmetic. There are only a handful of QWL programs in Canada through which workers have real decision-making power (e.g., Shell of Sarnia).[38] Senior management has not supported effective QWL because the program is perceived as threatening its control, and organized labour is concerned about QWL undermining the collective-bargaining process.[39] In fact, the OFL successfully lobbied to kill the provincial government-funded QWL centre.

In Western Europe and the Scandinavian countries, QWL is very extensive having the support of labour, management, and government. The Canadian experience differs: Like employee share-ownership, QWL is motivated by a desire to improve productivity, but without the principal owners and management surrendering either corporate control or control over lower levels of management.

Effective corporate control has been achieved by workers in only a small number of Canadian businesses. These "exceptions" are such a small subset of the Canadian economy that neither their assets nor their sales can account for even a decimal point of the total economy. Nevertheless, they are important because like all experiments, they represent a window to the future. The results will be studied by corporate planners, labour leaders, and governments and could influence the direction of the movements for employee ownership and workplace democracy.

The Worker Co-operative

Businesses which are owned in total and democratically controlled by their workers are usually referred to as worker co-operatives. This model for organizing work is not new, but it is one that has attracted interest in recent years.

It is believed that the first worker co-operative was started in Rochdale, England, in 1854, when a group of workers (the "Rochdale pioneers") set up a cotton mill, the Rochdale Co-operative Manufacturing Society.[40] Inspired by Robert Owen, the successful industrialist turned social innovator, the Rochdale pioneers established a set of principles that had previously guided a consumer co-operative they had created.

With respect to the worker co-operative, the most essential principle was that each member had one vote regardless of his or her investment in the business (though more often than not the members equally shared the financial risk). Education was a priority because as both workers and owners, members were responsible for the business both at the board level, where they democratically elected their representatives, and in the day-to-day operations, where they participated in decision-making (i.e., workplace democracy). The business gave priority to labour over capital insofar as investors received only a limited return on capital and did not receive voting rights; and any year-end surplus was allocated as a dividend to members on the basis of labour contribution.

The initial business, the cotton mill, was successful, and its worker-owners decided to expand. Lacking capital, they turned to outside investors and permitted them to become shareholders with voting rights. This proved to be an error because the outside shareholders (1200) out-voted the worker-owners (200) and eventually converted the enterprise to private ownership.[41] This need for capital has proven to be one of the major problems in developing worker co-operatives.

Notwithstanding this initial setback, the Rochdale pioneers

inspired others who took up the idea. In Canada, there have been numerous experiments, from as early as the 1860s and particularly in the 1880s because of the Knights of Labour.[42] As of 1987, it is estimated that there are nearly 400 worker co-ops in Canada, most developed in the 1980s, with about $300 million of sales and 15,000 members.[43] About two-thirds of Canadian worker co-ops are located within the province of Québec, where forestry co-ops in particular have a strong tradition and represent 10 per cent of forestry sales.[44] Nationally, forestry co-ops represent more than half of worker co-op sales, assets, and members. With the exception of the forestry sector, most worker co-ops are very small retail and service enterprises located in low-paid sectors of the economy.

Much of the current interest for developing worker co-operatives in Canada comes from their recent success in the Basque region of Spain.[45] In a 30-year period, the Mondragon group (as the Basque co-ops are called) has developed a system that now includes Spain's largest manufacturer of household appliances (ULGOR). In total, there are 172 co-operatives (94 industrial), with nearly 20,000 members and $2 billion sales in 1987.[46]

The heart of the Mondragon system is the Caja Laboral Popular (the working people's bank), a credit co-operative with assets of $2 billion and branches throughout the Basque country. The system also has its own educational institutions, a research and development organization (Ikerlan), a social-service system (Lagun-Aro), housing co-ops, and a consumer retail co-op (EROSKI). In other words, Mondragon is more than some worker co-operatives: It is a co-operative community.

There is a cultural and religious overlay to the Mondragon movement that probably means the total approach is not transferable to other countries.[47] The system was inspired by a parish priest, Don José María Arizmendi-Arrieta, who had studied the ideas of Robert Owen and the Rochdale pioneers. The Mondragon system also has been driven by Basque nationalism and by opposition to oppression from Franco's Spain. (The Basques sided with the losing Republican coalition during the 1930s' civil war.)

Some features of the Mondragon approach are being picked up in other countries, including Canada, because they represent practical solutions to problems that other worker co-operatives have faced over the years. Before the advent of the Mondragon co-ops, worker co-operatives were of two primary types -- non-share and share capital -- each of which was beset with problems that affected development.

Non-share worker co-operatives, for example, in Great Britain and Eastern Europe, shun equity investments by members as a means of financing.[48] This policy is based on the view that member equity creates a capitalist dynamic with greater concern about share values than the conditions of work. Non-share co-ops have financed their development primarily through loans and retained earnings. Some disadvantages to this approach are: The co-op can be burdened with a lot of debt, the repayment of which is a financial drain; the ability of a co-op to raise financing is hindered by a lack of member investment; and a non-share structure provides a disincentive for members to retain the enterprise's earnings for modernizing equipment, etc., because such investments become social property over which workers have no claim.[49] The non-share approach actually creates an incentive for workers to take high salaries and bonuses, a policy that in a competitive market may hinder a company's development. Not having shares is particularly unfair to founding members of the co-operative because even though their labour has contributed to building up the business, they receive no benefit other than salaries, which were probably low during the early years.

An alternative to the non-share worker co-operative, and one that has been used traditionally, requires that members purchase shares. In these share-capital co-operatives, outgoing members normally sell their shares to incoming members at whatever price the market will bear. In a successful company, the price of the member's investment can become very high. As a result these co-ops can have difficulty in recruiting new members and often either become dependent on hired labour or are sold to private owners.[50] This latter circumstance is most likely if a group of members coming to retirement are going to have difficulty realizing the proper value for their shares through a sale to new members.

Forestry co-operatives in the United States and in Canada have encountered these difficulties,[51] as have worker co-operatives in Israel and Western Europe.[52] As a solution to this problem, some Israeli worker co-ops in the trucking industry, are splitting shares and requiring that new members buy only a portion of the shares held by older members.[53] Both on philosophical and practical grounds, this type of share-capital co-operative model has been found wanting.

By comparison to these other models, the Mondragon co-operatives permit members to realize equity in their company, but retain the initial investment at a relatively constant level (the equivalent to the annual salary of the lowest paid member), thereby making membership just as accessible to new members as to the founders. Members also benefit from the development of their enterprise, both from increased earnings and dividends from any year-end surplus that are proportionate to their labour contribution. Both the initial investment and the dividends are allocated to a member's account where they collect interest at six per cent cumulative and are retained within the co-operative until the member leaves. In this way, the members realize the value of their labour, and the co-operative can use this money for development. The incentive to take high salaries is reduced because each member will eventually have claim on his or her account.

Interpreting Mondragon

The Mondragon approach has been interpreted within a broad conceptual framework in a series of papers by economist David Ellerman.[54] These papers are extremely important because they attempt to come to grips with the differences between worker co-operatives and privately-owned companies, including those with employee ownership. Drawing primarily on the classical liberal tradition (e.g., John Stuart Mill), Ellerman argues that the members in a worker co-operative have rights that are "personal" and "inalienable" much like the rights of citizens in a political democracy. By comparison, rights in a conventional corporation, including one with employee ownership, are associated with property holdings.

Ellerman refers to two types of rights: voting and profit. In a worker co-operative, each member has one vote regardless of his or her property in the enterprise. This vote -- a right of membership -- can be exercised at annual general meetings, elections to the board of directors, and in other decisions as decided by the co-operative. When a member leaves the co-operative, he or she ceases to have this voting right; that is, the right to vote is accorded only to those who work in the co-operative.

Similarly, the right to share in any year-end surplus (i.e., profit) or the responsibility for any year-end loss is also associated with work in the enterprise. Like salary, which is an advanced estimate of what the co-operative can afford to pay for each member's work, dividends are paid for labour according to an agreed-upon formula (e.g., hours of work or in relation to salary). Ellerman writes:

> A worker co-operative is a democratic work-community, an industrial democracy, where the membership rights are non-saleable personal rights that are attached to the functional role of working in the company, i.e., that are assigned to workers. The workers have the voting and profit rights in a co-operative because they work there, not because they have 'bought' the rights.[55]

This feature of member rights differentiates the worker co-operative from a conventional corporation:

> In a conventional corporation, the membership rights are transferable property rights attached to the shares of stock. The shares may be sold to whomever has enough money to buy them and who is not otherwise connected with the company. Since the votes and profits are distributed on a per share basis, shareholders in an ordinary corporation will have the number of votes and portions of the profits equal to the number of shares owned.[56]

This same point applies to employee-owned corporations and also helps to explain why, when such companies become successful, employees are often eager to sell their shares to outside owners: There is no restriction on doing so.[57]

Ellerman takes his interpretation further, arguing that even though the members of a worker co-operative finance the enterprise both through their initial investment ("membership fee") and retained year-end surpluses, they are not owners:

> The workers are members, not owners. Worker co-operatives have worker-members, not employee-owners. Unlike a conventional corporation, a worker co-operative is not a piece of property. It is not privately owned, it is not publicly owned, and it is not even socially owned -- since it is not a piece of property to be owned at all. It is a democratic social institution.[58]

Ellerman's argument flies in the face of the usual labeling of members as worker-owners. In the Mondragon-style co-operatives, members own property, that property coming from three sources: their initial investment; their share of year-end surpluses retained in the business; and interest on their investment and retained dividends. Given this property to which each member has title, why the reluctance to describe the workers as owners? In Ellerman's view, the initial investment is simply "obligation of membership" analogous "to union dues."[59] Workers pay the equivalent of a year's salary in order to qualify for membership, but this investment does not make them owners.

Although this analogy could be made, one basic difference between union dues and an initial investment in a worker co-operative is that a due is not property belonging to a member, but is money paid for a service. By contrast, the investment in a co-operative remains the property of the member and accumulates interest. Unlike shares in a conventional corporation though, members of a Mondragon-type co-op are denied the normal ownership right of selling their shares for the market value. They also cannot benefit financially (other than having immediate access to their accounts) from the sale of the business. The net worth of the business after the payment of members' accounts and other liabilities is seen as a "collective account" or "collective reserve" that in the event of a sale goes to the government to assist other co-operatives.

Therefore, the property rights in a worker co-op differ significantly from a conventional corporation. However, given that members own a major portion of the property in the business (as held in their accounts) and given that members democratically control the business including its total assets, it seems too extreme to argue that members are not owners. Rather we shall use the label "collective ownership" for Mondragon-type worker co-operatives.

There is another feature of the Mondragon approach that extends beyond collective ownership of the assets in the individual co-op. The Mondragon co-ops are interdependent with each other and with the Caja Laboral Popular which, in turn, is embedded in the Basque community. These links are both informal and contractual. With respect to the link between the individual co-op and the Caja Laboral Popular, there is a "contract of association"[60] whereby the Caja finances the co-op, and the co-op in turn provides regular statements of performance and deposits its earnings in the Caja. Therefore, it also seems appropriate to label the Mondragon co-operatives as a form of "community ownership." This argument is reinforced by the fact that, as noted, in the event of dissolution of the co-operative, the collective reserve (i.e., that which remains after members' accounts are paid) remains within the co-operative community.

Community ownership is different from social ownership insofar as social ownership has been associated with state ownership. Community ownership involves ownership by a community, that is, a subgroup of society (in this case, the co-operative community). Both labels, collective ownership and community ownership, describe the Mondragon approach, and both labels seem appropriate to similar worker co-operatives in other countries.

There is another point in Ellerman's interpretation that merits analysis. Ellerman implies that members of a worker co-operative have rights *as workers* which are fundamentally different from those of workers in a conventional corporation. Here, we are excluding the ownership rights (i.e., profit and corporate control) and are referring to the conditions of work. In principle this point is well taken. Worker co-operatives ought to be paragons of workplace democracy; because the workers are owners, the general working conditions ought to be ideal. The practice, however, is influenced by the overall social context, and may therefore deviate from the principle. For example, some worker co-ops (including the Mondragon co-ops) have been criticized for maintaining traditional management practices,[61] and as noted, some conventionally-owned companies are experimenting with participatory decision-making. Size is an important factor in creating a democratic workplace. Small worker co-operatives tend to be most successful in achieving working conditions which are consistent with democratic principles. Once a large number of workers are involved, the quality of participation in worker co-operatives may decline and bear greater similarity to conventionally-owned corporations.

There are other important rights for workers (e.g., minimum wage, hours of work, severance, health and safety conditions, etc.) that pertain to workers in all businesses, including worker-owned businesses. These rights, won through political organizing and negotiation, are enshrined in labour codes, charters of rights, and constitutions and are part of the civil liberties and human rights of all citizens in a society. It is not clear that workers in a worker co-operative come out ahead in these areas. Also, the dynamics of a worker-owned enterprise may lead to hardships that workers in conventionally-owned businesses do not experience. As owners of an enterprise, it is in the self-interest of workers to make sure that a sufficient portion of revenue is invested in their business. Therefore, they may be more willing to make sacrifices (referred to as "sweat equity") than the workers in a conventional business. For example, workers in Mondragon co-operatives agreed to a 14 per cent reduction in their purchasing power between 1979 and 1984 in order to finance a major modernization of their industries.[62] They were also compensated to a degree by labour dividends from year-end surpluses allocated to their accounts.

Or to use a Canadian example, Victoria Plywood Co-op was a workers' buyout of a Canadian Pacific Industries subsidiary. The co-op and the union, the International Woodworkers of America, were involved in a bitter dispute that led to decertification of the bargaining unit because the workers agreed to a large wage reduction (from $15 to $8 per hour) and a three-year wage freeze in order to obtain financing for the buyout.[63]

The issue of rights in a worker co-operative and a conventional corporation is more complex than Ellerman's formulation. As owners, a co-operative's members have important rights such as corporate control that workers in a conventional corporation normally lack. However, workers in conventional corporations have gained some rights through organizing themselves and through political struggles that are similar to the rights of workers in worker co-operatives.

Other Interpretations

In addition to the interpretation of workers' rights using classical liberal theory, worker-ownership can be analyzed within socialist and conservative frameworks. A key feature of the Mondragon model is the "socialization of the means of production," which are owned collectively by co-op members. Unlike a conventional business (with or without employee ownership), it is not possible for co-op members to profit from either the sale of their initial investment or the entire business. The co-operative is a social institution created for the purpose of providing jobs for its members.

The worker co-operative puts into practice the labour theory of value, first proposed by English economist David Ricardo and developed subsequently by Karl Marx.[64] (Ellerman uses a variation of this theory in his interpretation of Mondragon.) Both salaries and dividends represent a return on labour. They differ only insofar as salaries represent immediate earnings whereas dividends are allocated at year-end and members may have to await retirement before they are actually paid out. (Some worker co-ops limit the number of years that allocated dividends can be retained.)

By contrast, in a conventional corporation, dividends from profit are paid to shareholders whose claim is based solely on capital or property held in the company. The amount paid to shareholders affects the return for labour if the shareholders are non-workers (as is normally the case). Even more fundamentally, in a worker co-operative the decision about relative balance between these various types of earnings is made by workers. Therefore, workers not only control the means of production but also control the surplus value.

Socialized wealth in the Mondragon-type co-operatives differs fundamentally in form from the Soviet bloc countries where the state normally owns the means of production, albeit in the name of the workers. There is another fundamental difference: unlike Soviet state-enterprises, Mondragon co-ops are very accountable to the market. Their development is guided by a combination of business forces, state controls, and consumer demand -- the same forces that influence capitalist companies. Like entrepreneurs in general, worker-owners put capital at risk, their enterprise has business competitors, and they rely on consumer demand in order to succeed. They are, in the words of Adams and Hansen, "labour entrepreneurs."[65]

The market mix (the relative influence of business, state, and consumers) varies according to the country. In the United States, Britain, and Canada, for example, the business influence is relatively strong. In countries with a social democratic tradition (e.g., in Western Europe), there is relatively more state influence.

The adaptability of worker co-ops to a market-based economy has led to a conservative interpretation as workers' capitalism.[66] In spite of an entrepreneurial component, it seems inappropriate to describe as capitalist an enterprise in which surplus value is allocated to labour and in which residual assets revert to the co-operative community in the event of a dissolution. The capitalist interpretation seems more appropriate for companies with employee share-ownership plans. Rather, the Mondragon co-ops are best interpreted as a synthesis of classical liberalism and socialism in which workers have democratic rights, including control of both surplus value and the means of production. Within this embryonic system there is a reciprocity between industrial development and community development insofar as the community finances and supports the creation of worker-owned businesses, but these businesses are also beholden to the community in providing jobs and services. Mondragon represents workers' control and community control in partnership with the state, but with the state's involvement at a reduced level from the mixed economies of the West because the co-op system provides its own social welfare (e.g., unemployment compensation, healthcare, pensions).

Mondragon co-ops, like co-ops in general, function within a

capitalist economy but not necessarily by choice. It might also be possible to develop a system of worker co-operatives (perhaps not exactly like Mondragon) in an economy with greater state-control as the Soviets are attempting under perestroika. The adaptability of Mondragon, however, downplays its significance as a unique partnership between workers, a local community, and the state.[67] The Mondragon system is evolving within a capitalist structure and at the same time is casting an image that has the potential to change that structure.

Yet there is a paradox about this process that applies even more so to development of worker co-operatives in Canada. Like businesses in general, worker co-operatives require the political support of the state. Conventional businesses have been very adept at lobbying the state for grants, tax incentives, and favourable forms of regulation because the state also depends upon their capital to sustain the economy. For worker co-operatives, gaining support is more of a problem because at this point the network is too weak to create a formidable political alliance. Unlike conventional corporations, worker co-ops lack a big stick (i.e., capital) and significant power groups have yet to be attracted by the carrot.

The Political Context

One difficulty in the struggle to gain support is the "political ambiguity" of worker co-operatives. Ambiguity has led to some support from individuals of all political stripes, but an embrace from no major party. Among Conservatives, the worker co-operative has been advocated by Britain's Minister of Industry and Trade in the Thatcher Cabinet, Kenneth Clark, who has assisted an attempt to build a Mondragon system in Middlesbrough.[68] In Canada, between 1987 and 1988, the Conservative federal government approved three grants totaling more than $2 million for resource groups in Nova Scotia, [69] Québec,[70] Ontario, and Manitoba.[71] By government standards this level of financing is very small; nevertheless, it indicates some cabinet support for worker co-operatives.

Among liberals, the government of Prince Edward Island initiated a small financial-support program for worker co-ops in

1988.[72] The Liberal government of Québec also has maintained, at a reduced level from the previous Parti Québécois government, financial assistance for both development costs and resource groups.[73]

Stronger support has come from Canada's social democratic parties. As noted, Québec's Parti Québécois initiated a program in 1984 that led to the creation of a province-wide network of resource groups. Shortly afterwards, the NDP government of Manitoba created a support program that has not been altered by the Conservative government elected in 1988.[74] Also, the federal NDP is on record as supporting worker co-operatives as part of a community economic development strategy.[75] There is reason to believe that the worker co-op would fit comfortably within a social-democratic development strategy if the worker co-op became a credible alternative.

The political ambiguity of worker co-operatives has also affected the attitude of significant power groups in society. The conventional corporate community, the primary power group in Canada, has no interest in worker co-operatives. Successful worker-owned companies such as Lamford Forest Products are simply perceived as a type of employee share-ownership.[76] Indeed, this perception is often shared by worker-owners themselves, even if they use a co-operative structure.

Among co-operative corporations there is greater support because many of the advocates of worker co-operatives are involved in other types of co-ops. However, in spite of this association, the mainstream of the co-operative movement has been lukewarm to this model of organizing work. Canadian co-operatives are not a unified movement, but separate movements (i.e., primary producers, consumers, tenants, credit-union users) with weak links through their political voice, the Canadian Co-operative Association (CCA).[77] Since the first loyalty of the various organizations is to their members rather than the movement, there is a limit to which the leaders of consumer co-operatives, for example, will lobby on behalf of worker co-operatives. There is also a limit to the political clout of the co-operative sector in Canada. It does embrace about 12 million members and more than $68 billion of assets.[78] Yet in relative terms, its assets are small at about 2.5 per cent of the GNP.

The CCA has, nevertheless, taken some significant initiatives in support of worker co-operatives. The initiatives have included featuring the worker co-operative in a 1984 task-force report, which was submitted to the federal cabinet by the forerunner to the CCA, the Co-operative Union of Canada.[79] That report referred to worker co-operatives as "an idea whose time as come." Subsequently, the CCA funded a small project to lobby government on behalf of worker co-operative organizations and recently created an advisory group for interested volunteers from the established co-operatives.[80] It also has "fronted" funding applications to government on behalf of worker co-operative development groups, advocated that the government fund five such groups in English Canada, and made worker co-operatives an election priority in 1988.[81]

This support does not necessarily reach down to the grassroots of Canadian co-operatives. In part this is because in the vast majority of co-operatives, the workers are employees, much like employees in conventional corporations, and the labour relations are not always exemplary. When the large consumer co-operatives in Saskatchewan are compared to privately-owned supermarkets, for example, there are fewer unions and more strikes in the co-operatives.[82]

Although the worker co-operative has roots within the co-operative tradition, it is not overly compatible with other co-operative models. A few co-operatives (e.g., the Co-operators Group which includes Co-operators Insurance) have experimented with a structure which includes the workers as one stakeholder within the multi-stakeholder co-operative (see Chapter 5).[83] Also some housing co-operatives are developing worker co-operatives to provide services to that movement.[84] In general, though, the attitude of the co-operative movement has been to view the worker co-operative as another co-operative model which will stand or fall on its own merits. To assist it, the CCA and some other co-operatives (e.g., Co-op Atlantic, the Co-operative Housing Foundation) are providing small amounts of tactical support.

Organized Labour

If worker co-operatives are to become a significant part of the Canadian economy, they will require the support of organized labour. At present, there is no general position from organized labour. There are some advocates and some opponents, but for most unionists the worker co-operative is peripheral to their primary agenda. The worker co-op is not found among public service organizations nor in most large industries where unions predominate. Also, the synthesis between workers and owners is foreign to labour. Organized labour remains committed to bargaining on behalf of workers against owners as in the conventional business organization. There is concern that worker-owners would stand apart from ordinary employees, thereby dividing the movement.

Yet organized labour has been forced to consider worker buyouts as a defence against the large number of plant shutdowns. In these circumstances, the response to the closing depends both upon the particular union and the viability of the business. One of Québec's large labour federations, the Confederation des syndicats nationaux (CSN) has established an advisory group to assist selected groups to organize worker-owned enterprises;[85] the Québec Federation of Labour is permitting worker co-op members to take advantage of the tax credits in its solidarity fund (a venture-capital fund) and has agreed to invest a small portion of that fund in worker co-ops;[86] the International Woodworkers have assisted one workers' buyout and opposed another;[87] and the president of the Ontario Federation of Labour, Gordon Wilson, recently criticized "Liberal and Conservative governments" for "standing in the way of some willing workers who wanted to buy out the business they worked for."[88]

The rhetoric is becoming more positive but not exclusively so. In its brief to the MacDonald Commission on the Canadian economy, the United Auto Workers (now the Canadian Auto Workers) states:

> The issue of employee buyouts has received a great deal of publicity. Again, we are less than enthusiastic. In exceptional circumstances, workers with no other choices may decide to risk this direction, but these remain exceptions. They are

certainly not a panacea in any broader way. It simply does not make sense for workers with limited savings to risk an investment in operations which businesses find too risky and in which the market already rejected.[89]

Although other labour organizations have more positive rhetoric than the Canadian Auto Workers, the term "exceptional circumstances" is an appropriate descriptor for Canadian labour's support. In Italy and France, organized labour has successfully participated in supporting a broad range of buyouts and start-ups.[90] At present Canadian labour is highly selective. Only in Québec has labour's support been more general, and only in Québec is there significant worker co-op development.

The cause-effect relationships are complex; organized labour in Québec has been influenced by the growing number of worker co-ops, and because of that, has viewed worker ownership as an alternative worthy of active support. Like the labour movement in general, Québec unions evaluate worker co-operatives in terms of increasing their membership and a general vision of economic democracy.

Outside of Québec, worker co-ops are small in number. Recently there have been some notable successes: Lamford;[91] Vancouver's CRS,[92] the largest wholesaler of natural foods in Canada; Winnipeg's Vent-Air buyout;[93] Toronto's Big Carrot natural foods;[94] and Prince Edward Island's potato-chip production co-op.[95] Others could be mentioned, though in the context of the second-largest country in the world (a country balkanized by strong regional loyalties and linguistic divisions), these successes are quite isolated. Yet successes are needed before powerful groups like organized labour will seriously consider the worker co-op.

Historical Parallels

There is a parallel in Canada between the current state of worker co-ops and that of non-profit co-operative housing in the late 1960s and early 1970s (as indicated in a useful analysis by Mark Goldblatt).[96] At that time, housing co-operatives were relatively isolated developments initiated by members. These pioneers convinced significant power groups in society that the idea was viable. When land and housing prices spiraled between

1973 and 1974, a coalition of the Canadian Labour Congress, the United Church, the Co-operative Union of Canada, and the Co-operative Housing Foundation approached the Federal government. Their timing was fortuitous because there was a left-leaning government of Liberals propped up by the NDP.

The lobbyists were able to establish a financial-support program for co-op housing that resulted in government underwriting a portion of the development costs and in providing subsidies for low-income members. From there a network of development groups sprung up across the country and many housing co-ops have followed, until at present there are more than 125,000 members.[97] Although private housing developers have lobbied against the program, achieving cutbacks in the early 1980s,[98] the future looks bright and current development is unprecedented.

It is unclear whether the political chemistry that led to the take-off of co-op housing in 1974 can be re-created for worker co-ops. Arguably, the problems in developing worker co-ops are more extreme because a competitive market means that an existing co-op may be forced to close. Housing co-ops, once established, endure. The members of worker co-ops are expected to take considerable financial risks. In the early years of the business there may be insufficient revenues to pay good salaries and even if the business succeeds, there is no guarantee that earnings will exceed the rate for jobs in similar types of markets. Housing co-ops, by comparison, require no member investment and have low housing charges compared to the rental market. In spite of these differences, there are also obvious parallels: social needs that are not being met through conventional institutions, a growing number of successful examples, small amounts of support from powerful groups in society, a network of dedicated activists, and a lobbying process for a fair share of the state's resources available for business development.

The ambiguity of worker co-ops can be a handicap because political groups are uncertain whether the co-operative approach is useful to them. But, under circumstances in which existing political orientations are not meeting social needs, there is greater openness to new syntheses as represented by worker co-ops. Today the business community finds itself under tremendous competitive pressure and is looking at employee share-ownership as a method of increasing productivity. The business community has been successful in lobbying the state for tax credits and grants that are encouraging small employee-share purchases.

The social needs addressed through worker co-operatives -- high levels of unemployment in specific regions, closings of potentially profitable plants, the desire for workers' control, the search for meaning through work -- are no less important than those raised by the conventional business community. An important part of convincing power groups in society that the worker co-operative is worthy of support is the creation of a sound strategy for development. We now turn our energies to that task.

Notes

[1]Joe Dangor, "Workers of Canada Unite to Buy their Own Companies," *Small Business*, October 1987, p. 8.

[2]William Annett, "Brother, Can You Spare a Sawmill?" *Small Business*, December 1987, pp. 34-40.

[3]Keith Bradley and Alan Gelb, *Worker Capitalism: The New Industrial Relations* (Cambridge, Ma.: MIT Press, 1983), pp. 1-61.

[4]*Employee Share-Ownership at Canada's Public Corporations* (Toronto: The Toronto Stock Exchange, 1987), p. 6.

[5]*Employee Share-Ownership at Canada's Public Corporation*, p. 40.

[6]Richard Long, "Employee Ownership: The North American Experience," Paper Presented at the Conference on Future Perspectives in Industrial Democracy, Dubrovnik, Yugoslavia, October 3, 1983, pp. 20-21.

[7]*Employee Stock-Ownership Plans: Little Evidence on Corporate Performance* (Gaithersburg, Maryland: General Accounting Office, 1988).

[8]*Employee Share-Ownership at Canada's Public Corporations*, p. 55.

[9]Jonathan Ferguson, "Stronach's Proposition Leaves Turner in a Bind," *The Toronto Star*, January 23, 1988, p. C3. See also Bruce Livesay, "Magna's Millions: Keeping the Factory Union-Free," *Our Times*, March 1987, p. 17.

[10]Kenneth Kidd, "Canadian Tire Workers Vote 85 Per Cent in Favour of Planned Restructuring," *The Toronto Star*, February 18, 1988, pp. Dl, D4.

[11] *Employee Share-Ownership at Canada's Public Corporations*, p. 36.

[12]Vaughan Lyon, "Ontario Share-Purchase Plan Opposed by Organized Labour, *Worker Co-op*, 6, No. 3 (1986), 6-7.

[13]Ruth Seeley, "Ontario's Proposed Employee Share-Ownership Plan Does not Fit the Bill," *Small Business*, June 1987, p. 8.

[14]Corey Rosen, "U.S. Tax Law Encourages Employee Ownership," *Worker Co-op*, 6, No. 3 (1987), 6-8.

[15]Rosen, "U.S. Tax Law," pp. 6-8.

[16]"ESOP Growth Strong in 1987," *The Employee Ownership Report*, VIII, No. 5 (1988), 1.

[17]"United States, Around the World," *Worker Co-op*, Winter 5, No. 3 (1985), 35-36.

[18]"We Try Harder! (The AVIS Buyout)," *Worker Co-op*, 7, No. 3 (1988), 21-22.

[19]Susan Dentzer, "The Foibles of ESOPs," *Newsweek*, October 19, 1987, 59.

[20]Dentzer, "The Foibles of ESOPs," pp. 59-60.

[21]Lynn Williams, *Labour Unions and Employee Ownership* (Pittsburg: United Steelworkers of America, 1985).

[22]Rosen, "U.S.Tax Law," pp. 6-8.

[23]Weirton Joint Study Committee, *Weirton Steel Corporation*, August 1983, 86 pp.

[24]Louis Kelso and Mortimer Adler, *The Capitalist Manifesto* (Westport, Conn.: Greenwood, 1975), 265 pp.

[25]Hon. Russell B. Long, "Employee Ownership and Better Labour-Management Relations, *Congressional Record*, June 29, 1984, p. 7.

[26]"Legislative Outlook for Employee Ownership," *The Employee Ownership Report*, 3, No. l (1988), p. 4.

[27]Rosen, "U.S. Tax Law," pp. 6-8.

[28]Rosen, "U.S. Tax," p. 7.

[29]Denis Clark and Merry Guben, *Future Bread* (Philadelphia: O & O Investment Fund, 1985).

[30]"Legislative Outlook for Employee Ownership," p. 4.

[31]*Temiskaming*, National Film Board of Canada, 1975.

[32]Jack Quarter, "There's More than Beef at the Beef Terminal, *Worker Co-op*, 3, No. 2 (1983), 6-7. In 1987 the Beef Terminal went into receivership.

[33]"Canadian Tire Ruling, *Worker Co-op*, 7, No. 2 (1987), 32.

[34]*Employee Share-Ownership at Canada's Public Corporations*, p. 55.

[35]*Employee Share-Ownership at Canada's Public Corporations*, p. 48.

[36]*QWL Focus: New Technology and Organizational Choice* (Toronto: QWL Centre, Ministry of Labour, 1988), 60pp.

[37]Edward Trist, *The Evolution of Socio-Technical Systems* (Toronto: QWL Centre, Ministry of Labour, 1988).

[38]Norman Halpern, *Sociotechnical Systems Design: The Shell Sarnia Experience* (mimeo).

[39]United Auto Workers, "Can Canada Compete?" in *The Other MacDonald Report*, ed. D. Drache and D. Cameron (Toronto: Lorimer, 1985), p. 152.

[40]Robert Oakeshott, *The Case for Workers' Co-ops* (London: Routledge and Kegan Paul, 1978), p. 55.

[41]Oakeshott, *The Case for Workers' Co-ops*, p. 56.

[42]Ian Macpherson, "Reflections on the Uneven History of Worker Co-operatives in Canada, *Worker Co-op*, 6, No.4 (1987), 8-10.

[43]Alain Roy, *Workers' Co-operatives: The Canadian Scene* (Ottawa: Co-op Secretariat, June 1988), 22 pp.

[44]Alain Côté, "Ten Thousand Québec Workers Try Another Way," *Worker Co-op*, 6, No. 1 (1986), 8-9.

[45]Oakeshott, *The Case for Workers' Co-ops*, Chapter 10; Henk Thomas and Chris Logan, *Mondragon: An Economic Analysis* (London: Allen and Unwin, 1982); and Alistair Campbell, Charles Keen, Geraldine Norman and Robert Oakeshott, *Worker-Owners: The Mondragon Achievement* (London: Anglo-German Foundation, 1977), 66 pp.

[46]"Mondragon,"*Worker Co-op*, 7, No. 2 (1987), 25.

[47]*Mondragon Co-operatives: Myth or Model?* (Milton Keynes: Open University, 1981), 122 pp.

[48]Oakeshott, *The Case for Workers' Co-ops*, Chapter 10.

[49]David Ellerman, "Comments on Quarter's Review," *Worker Co-op*, 5, No. 4 (1986), 4-5.

[50]David Ellerman, "Worker Co-operatives: The Question of Legal Structure," in *Worker Co-operatives in America*, ed. R. Jackall and H. Levin (Berkeley: University of California Press, 1984), pp. 268-269.

[51]Katrina Berman, "The Worker-Owned Plywood Co-operatives," in *Workplace Democracy and Social Change*, ed. F. Lindenfeld and J. Rothschild-Whitt (Boston: Porter-Sargent, 1982), pp. 161-176.

[52]Jack Quarter, "Worker Co-operatives in Israel," *Worker Co-op*, 5, No. 2 (1985), 18.

[53]"Making Membership Affordable, *Worker Co-op*, 7, No. 2 (1987), 30.

[54]David Ellerman, "What Is a Worker Co-operative?" Somerville: Industrial Co-operative Association, 1982, p. 1; David Ellerman, "Worker Co-operatives: The Question of Legal Structure," pp. 257-273; and David Ellerman and Peter Pitegoff, "The Democratic Corporation: The New Worker Co-operative Statute in Massachusetts," *Review of Law and Social Change*, XI, No. 3 (1982-83), 441-472.

[55]Ellerman, "What Is a Worker Co-operative?" p. 1.

[56]Ellerman, "What Is a Worker Co-operative?" p. 1.

[57]For an example, see Bob Schutte, "The Pioneer Chainsaw Massacre: The Bitter Lessons of a Plant Shutdown," *Worker Co-op*, 5, No. 3 (1985), 14-15.

[58]Ellerman, "Worker Co-operatives: The Question of Legal Structure," p. 267.

[59]Ellerman, "Comments on Quarter's Review," pp. 4-5.

[60]Oakeshott, *The Case for Worker Co-ops*, p. 199.

[61]Anna Gutierrez Johnson and William Foote Whyte, "The Mondragon System of Worker Production Co-operatives," in *Workplace Democracy and Social Change*, p. 188. According to a more recent book on Mondragon, there is now more worker participation in decision-making. See William Whyte and Kathleen Whyte, *Making Mondragon* (New York: ILR Press, 1988).

[62]Lankide Aurrezkia, *The Mondragon Experiment* (Mondragon: Caja Laboral Popular, 1986), p. 4.

[63]Dana Weber, "Victoria Plywood Plant Restructured as a Worker Co-op," *Worker Co-op*, 5, No. 1 (1985), 9.

[64]Karl Marx, "Critique of the Gotha Program." in *Marx and Engels Basic*

Writings on Politics and Philosophy, ed. S. Feuer (New York: Anchor, 1959), pp. 112-132.

[65]Frank Adams and Gary Hansen, *Putting Democracy to Work* (Eugene, Oregon: Hulogosi, 1987), p. 39.

[66]Bradley and Gelb, *Worker Capitalism*, Chapter 5.

[67]William Whyte and Kathleen Whyte, *Making Mondragon*

[68]Norma Henderson, "Mondragon, U.K.," *Worker Co-op*, 7, No. 2 (1988), 26.

[69]Grant MacDonald, "Pilot Project Starts," *Worker Co-op*, 6, No. 3 (1987), 32.

[70]Claude Carbonneau, "Feds Cough Up $1.6 million for Québec Development Groups," *Worker Co-op*, 8, No. 1 (1988), 13-14.

[71]Albert Chambers, "CCA Nicks Innovations for $249,300 Buyouts Project," *Worker Co-op*, 8, No. 1 (1988), 7.

[72]Frank Driscoll, "Prince Edward Island Worker Co-op Program," *Worker Co-op*, 7, No. 4 (1988), 28.

[73]Jacques LaRue, "Why Québec is so Successful in Developing Worker Co-operatives," *Worker Co-op*, 6, No. 2 (1986), 42.

[74]Doug Davison, "Manitoba's Employment Co-operative Program is off and Running, *Worker Co-op*, 5, No. 3 (1985), 18-19.

[75]Ernie Epp, "A Canadian Program for Community Economic Development," (mimeo).

[76]Annett, "Brother Can You Spare a Sawmill," pp. 34-40.

[77]G. Melnyk, *The Search for Community* (Montréal: Black Rose, 1986), 170 pp.

[78]*Co-operatives Canada '87* (Ottawa: Canadian Co-operative Association, 1987), 33 pp.

[79]*Report of the National Task Force on Co-operative Development* (Ottawa: Canadian Co-operative Association, 1984).

[80]Albert Chambers and Mark Goldblatt, "CCA," *Worker Co-op*, 7, No. 4 (1988), 18.

[81]Albert Chambers, "CCA Makes Worker Co-ops an Election Priority," *Worker Co-op*, 8, No. 2 (1988), 24.

[82]K.W. Wetzel and D.G. Gallagher, "Union-Management Labour Relations in Co-operatives," Unpublished Paper, 1986, p. 4.

[83]Teunis Haalboom and John Jordan, "The Multi-Stakeholder Co-operative," *Worker Co-op*, 6, No.3 (1987), 10-14.

[84]Dana Weber, "Housing Co-ops Learn about Worker Co-ops," *Worker Co-op*, 7, No. 4 (1988), 9.

[85]Leopold Beaulieu, "Major Québec Labour Federation Starts Organizing Worker Co-operatives, *Worker Co-op*, 6, No. 3 (1987), 20-21.

[86]Albert Chambers, "February 1988 Budget," *Worker Co-op*, 7, No. 4 (1988), 18.

[87]Dana Weber, "A Union Viewpoint on Forestry Buyouts in B.C.," *Worker Co-op*, 5, No. 4 (1986), 12-14.

[88]Gordon Wilson, "Address to the Toronto NDP Convention," April 30, 1988, p. 7.

[89]United Auto Workers, "Can Canada Compete?" p. 153.

[90]Oakeshott, *The Case for Workers' Co-ops*, Chs. 8-9.

[91]Annett, "Brother Can You Spare a Sawmill?" pp. 34-40.

[92]Melanie Conn and Dana Weber, "CRS May Be Number One in Western Canada," *Worker Co-op*, 7, No. 3 (1988), 23.

[93]Jeremy Hull, "Vent Air: Phoenix Is Rising," *Worker Co-op*, 7, No. 3 (1988), 36-37.

[94]Jack Quarter, "Mary Lou Morgan Dreams and The Big Carrot Grows," *Worker Co-op*, 7, No. 2 (1987), 22-24.

[95]Brian Iler, "Evangeline Worker Co-op a Success," *Worker Co-op*, 7, No. 3 (1988), 14.

[96]Mark Goldblatt, "Launching a Worker Co-op Sector: Lessons from Co-op Housing," *Worker Co-op*, 7, No. 4 (1988), 9-12.

[97]Joan Selby and Alexandra Wilson, *Canada's Housing Co-operatives: An Alternative Approach to Resolving Community Problems* (Ottawa: Co-op Housing Foundation, 1988).

[98]Jack Quarter, "Tories Must Define Policy on Co-op Housing," *Toronto Star*, June 25, 1985, op. ed. page.

Chapter 2

Starting Worker-Owned Enterprises: Problems and Prospects

Jack Quarter

Start-ups of worker co-operatives[1] have gone hand-in-hand with specialized "resource groups" committed to their development. Resource groups provide an infrastructure consisting of advocates and technical experts, and they assist in assembling the financial package -- the lifeblood of any new business.

Without specialized resource groups, worker co-operatives would still be created but not as rapidly. For example, between 1938 and 1983, approximately 202 worker co-ops were started in Québec.[2] Since the funding of a network of specialized resource groups (groupes-conseils) by the government in 1984, equivalent numbers of new worker co-ops have been started. In other words, development in the past three years with specialized resource groups equaled that of the previous 45 years. No doubt there were other factors that also accounted for the increase, but evidence from virtually every country with significant development in worker co-ops suggests that resource groups accelerate the pace of development.

Writing about the British experience, Chris Cornforth states: "One major factor in their growth has been the establishment of co-operative support organizations (CSOs) in many parts of the country."[3] Previous to the creation of the first CSO in 1976, there were only 36 worker co-ops in Britain. In the period 1984-86, with a network of 80 CSOs, about 200 new enterprises were developed each year.[4]

Without resource groups, there is little stimulus for development because workers are seldom motivated to become owners of the enterprise in which they work; and they rarely consider collective ownership. In part, this is because conventional business consultants do not encourage effective worker ownership (not to be confused with employee share-ownership). Consequently, resource groups fill this gap by steering prospective worker-owners toward the worker co-operative. Unlike conventional consultants, who are detached from the enterprises they assist, the members of resource groups enter into a symbiotic relationship with worker-owned enterprises, taking a leading role in their development, a role that in turn becomes the raison d'être for the resource groups. In other words, resource groups are an integral part of what they are creating. Initially, at least, they provide a new enterprise with such key components of entrepreneurship as business planning and market and financial analysis.

Like the movement itself, money (or the lack of it) is a fundamental problem for the resource groups because most worker-owned enterprises lack the revenue to pay the going rate for their services. Therefore, the resource groups have required some form of external funding for their consultants to earn an acceptable salary. In countries such as Canada and Britain, the funding has come from the government. Québec's network of groupe-conseils, for example, received government funding that permitted its staff to be salaried.[5] Britain's CSOs have been funded by municipal councils, usually labour controlled; but one project in Middlesbrough was funded by the Conservative national government.[6] Funding in the United States has come from large foundations and churches. When charged, fees-for-service are usually insufficient payment. If external funding is lacking, consultants draw very low incomes. This arrangement can be sustained for a while, but it does not bode well either for resource groups or for the movement to which they are linked.

An exception to this pattern is the consultants who have developed the Mondragon group of worker co-ops in the Basque region of Spain. As noted in Chapter 1, this highly successful system of primarily industrial enterprises has about 20,000 worker-owners and about $2 billion of sales.[7] The consultants' group which does the planning for each enterprise was originally housed in the central credit co-operative for the system (The Caja Laboral Popular). Recently, the consultants developed an arm's length relationship, becoming a separate empressarial division, though they remain employees of the Caja. But even in this highly successful system, the full cost of development is not borne by the members of a new co-operative. True, direct costs of development are assigned to a new co-op as an operating expense. Initially, though, these costs are covered by the Caja, as is the overhead for the consulting service. The overhead, which is costly, involves planning time for projects that prove to be non-feasible. (For every project that is feasible, nine others are not.)[8]

The development costs are recouped to an extent by the requirement ("contract of association") that each worker co-op deposit its savings in the Caja. But even with these deposits, the Caja's investments in worker co-operatives only break even. The system is subsidized through private-sector investments (65 per cent of the Caja's investments).[9]

Another feature of the Mondragon approach which sets it apart from the Canadian tradition is that development has been proactive or, in ideological terms, "top-down." The planning process from the initial market analysis through to organizing the business is co-ordinated by the business consultants of the Caja, who work with the leadership group of a new enterprise. By contrast, the Canadian tradition has been bottom-up or populist. The initiative for creating and developing worker-owned businesses has come from workers who seek the assistance of consultants if they can afford it. The consultants' role can be described as reactive -- that is, they respond to proposals from worker-owners. In Canada, the primary financing for development costs also comes from workers, although small loans from banks, credit unions, and private investors are often part of the package.

Both of these factors -- the pre-eminence of workers in the planning and the dominance of workers' shares in financing -- mean that most worker-owned businesses in Canada are small, underfinanced, and poorly planned operations with considerable risk of failure. Many of the new starts are marginal businesses with the members either working part-time because of low revenues or working irregularly because their service is seasonal.

In total, about 400 worker co-operatives are incorporated in Canada with about 15,000 members and $300 million in sales.[10,11] About two-thirds of the worker-owned enterprises are in Québec, and there are also noteworthy pockets in Manitoba and Nova Scotia. This sector is dominated by forestry co-ops, which represent more than half of members, sales, and assets.

In Nova Scotia, sales from that province's entire worker-owned sector total only $5 million.[12] Québec's worker-owned sector is more productive with sales of about $200 million.[13] However, almost 90 per cent of that business is being transacted by established forestry co-ops and by one printing business (Harpell). As in the rest of the country, the majority of Québec's worker-owned enterprises remain small, marginal businesses.

Even though there are worker co-operatives throughout Canada and an impressive number in Québec, the interconnectedness that signifies a movement is lacking. This shortcoming has both political and economic consequences. Politically, it has meant that the movement cannot speak for itself in lobbying governments but has had to create ersatz relationships with other organizations (such as the Canadian Co-operative Association) having a broader mandate. (An exception to this pattern is Québec's forestry co-ops, which have created a provincial and two regional associations.[14] Provincial associations of worker co-ops in Québec and Nova Scotia are still without a strong membership base.) The independence of worker co-operatives has denied them economies of scale in marketing, purchasing, and support services -- economies that reduce the risks of failure in a competitive market.

While independence may satisfy the social needs of members, insofar as they alone can shape their own house, it does not invite economic success. This point had been made by John Jordan in an earlier analysis of Canadian worker co-operatives, and it is equally apparent today.[15] The impact of this structural weakness should not be underestimated for either existing enterprises or the development of new ones.

Nevertheless, worker co-operatives in Canada appear to perform at least to the standard of small privately-owned enterprises in similar circumstances. For example, some research suggests that Québec's worker-owned enterprises are more productive than similar privately-owned businesses,[16] and that Nova Scotia's, New Brunswick's,[17] and Québec's[18] worker-owned enterprises have a lower failure rate than the small-business sector in general. Notwithstanding such evidence, there can be no doubt that like conventional small businesses, worker-owned enterprises have a very high risk of failure. The data from the Maritimes indicate that after nine years, 47 per cent have failed, and after 18 years, the toll climbs to 62 per cent. The Québec data are even more stark: The ten-year failure rate is 68 per cent, and after five years, 48 per cent.[19]

When one also considers that the incomes drawn by worker-owners in the start-up phase tend to be low and that hours can be long and self-exploitive, one can understand why working people and labour leaders are seldom attracted to worker-owned enterprises. In Canada, these enterprises have been started by committed and devoted idealists who often are less interested in starting just another business than in demonstrating that there is another way for a business to be organized.

The challenge is to create an approach to development which will assist the worker-ownership movement to overcome its marginal status. To do that, it would seem useful to analyze some approaches that have encountered greater success.

Proactive Approaches

As noted, the Mondragon group is the prime example of a successful approach to development. The strategy has been to plan medium-sized industries, with an investment per job of approximately $100,000.[20] The financial package is assembled from a combination of member investments of about $10,000 and financing (i.e., loans) from the Caja. It is anticipated that each new enterprise will break even within four years. During the period 1979-84, for example, business revenues from Mondragon industries increased by 200 per cent, and exports increased by 300 per cent.[21] During the decade 1974-84, Mondragon co-operatives increased their membership from 11,417 to 18,795. Over the same period, Spain was losing about 252,000 jobs per year, and the Basque region was losing about 23,800.[22] There has been only one business failure in the Mondragon group (in the 1950s),[23] and the co-op members have higher earnings than workers doing similar jobs in conventional industries.[24] Management, by comparison, receives less than it would in other businesses or in government. Unlike most worker-owned enterprises in Canada, Mondragon industries have provided secure, decent-paying jobs.

The Mondragon model has been criticized for insufficient workplace democracy and for using a traditional Taylorian approach to management.[25] In part, this is a problem of size: It is difficult to arrange for the same involvement in decision-making in an enterprise of 300 workers as in a small one with four or five. Whereas most worker-owned enterprises in Canada practice direct democracy (not always with ideal results), the Mondragon approach is, by necessity, based on representative democracy with the associated difficulties of non-involvement of the rank-and-file. Recently, Mondragon has attempted to design its industries so that there is a greater degree of worker participation in decision-making.[26] The Mondragon approach has also been criticized because the Caja has too much control. According to Chris Axworthy: "The ethos of the Caja resembles that of a stern parent. . . .The Caja acts as if it knows best what the individual co-operatives should do, want to do, and aspire to."[27]

The Caja provides the blueprint for the business, and it continues to monitor the progress of the business. The "patriarchal" role of the Caja is the price that is paid for the development model. If the workers planned their own business and arranged their own financing, then the Caja's role would be of less importance to them.

The shortcomings of the Mondragon system appear to be related to their centrally-controlled approach toward business planning and finance. However, there is no reason why a proactive approach to development, like Mondragon's, cannot include preparation of the members for a democratic workplace.

PACE, a Philadelphia-based resource group that specializes in the food industry, uses a variation of the Mondragon approach which includes the training of prospective co-op members for participation in a democratic workplace.[28,29] PACE is best known for developing a system of supermarkets (O&O stores) in the Philadelphia region. Appropriately then, PACE refers to itself as a "development group." Unlike the traditional resource group which reacts to proposals from prospective worker-owners, PACE has actively created the business plan though tailoring it to the needs of each community that wants an O&O store. The PACE approach recognizes that the skills required to plan a business professionally differ from those required to work in it.

PACE's specialization in the food industry permits its staff to acquire expertise in that sector. There is another advantage to the PACE approach: By replicating, with some modifications, an already successful business plan, PACE reduces the development cost, a large expense for a new business of any scope. (Mondragon has done the same by establishing worker-owned enterprises that assemble and market products developed by private industries -- e.g., Mitsubishi.)[30]

This process of replication has permitted PACE to create somewhat larger businesses than are normally started by worker-owners and to integrate these businesses within a system that now includes five retail outlets and a second-degree co-op that acts as a wholesaler and provides common services (e.g., accounting and member education).[31] Having such a system produces the economies of scale found in successful privately-owned enterprises, particularly franchises, and thereby reduces the risks of business failure. It is also noteworthy that organized labour has supported the O&O system.[32] The O&O stores, both the original buyouts and the starts, are unionized, having been supported from their inception by local 1357 of the United Food and Commercial Workers.

The PACE approach bears many similarities to Mondragon. Like Mondragon, the development group provides the framework for the system. The development group takes the lead in the initial planning and assists with ongoing R&D and related services. However, in the Mondragon approach, the framework is much broader than the development group. That entity is embedded in the Caja Laboral Popular that finances worker co-operatives. The co-operatives, in turn, participate in the community through becoming members of the consumer retail co-ops (EROSKI), the housing co-ops, and the co-op schools.

The Mondragon system involves an integrated co-operative community developing worker-owned enterprises. PACE, by comparison, does not have the integration with a co-operative financial system or the same degree of integration within a co-operative community -- in part because that co-operative community does not exist in the Philadelphia area. Therefore, to develop O&O stores, PACE has to interest local communities and workers who want this type of enterprise, and it has to turn to outside financial sources. The support system is much narrower than in Mondragon and must be arranged for each enterprise. Unlike Mondragon where the development costs are subsidized by the Caja, PACE lacks a financial arm to subsidize its projects. Therefore, it has had to rely on support from foundations and churches to offset costs of planning.[33]

The Canadian Context

In Canada there are very few examples of a proactive approach to developing worker co-operatives. One exception is the creation of the potato-chip production plant in Urbanville, Prince Edward Island.[34,35] This plant in the Acadian section of

P.E.I. was planned by the Evangeline co-op council, a regional association of co-operatives. Evangeline, a 20-square-kilometre area with 2,500 residents, is very special insofar as much of its economy is organized through 17 co-operatives.[36] Therefore, the idea of the community taking on responsibility for planning worker-owned industries is very natural.

The Caisse Populaire Evangeline provided member-loans to the worker-owners of the potato-chip plant and an interim grant of $225,000. The total financial package of $775,000 was put together from a number of government and community agencies, including the Baie Acadien Venture Capital Fund established by the credit union. Following approval of the business plan and arrangement of the financing, 14 worker-owners were recruited and trained for the business. At this point in time it is premature to evaluate the success of the business. Its first year did surpass expectations, and Evangeline community leaders are optimistic about its future.

Like Mondragon co-ops, the potato-chip plant is part of a community bound together by strong cultural and linguistic ties. Also like Mondragon, a credit co-operative -- the Evangeline Credit Union -- took the lead in planning and financing this development. The Evangeline co-operatives are not dominated by worker co-operatives as in Mondragon. There are consumer, producer (farmers, fish catchers), housing, and healthcare co-ops in the Evangeline group. Like Mondragon, though, these co-ops are part of a system with an umbrella organization (Conseil Co-op) and have ties to the credit union both through financing of their initial development and through using their deposits to finance subsequent development.

The "contract of association" between the Evangeline group and the credit union is less explicit than in Mondragon, as are the ties between individual co-ops. Nevertheless, both Mondragon and Evangeline are a system of co-operatives within a community with strong cultural ties, and in both cases a credit co-operative takes the lead in planning and financing -- or what Axworthy refers to as "parenting."

Exceptions to the Rule

There are a number of very successful worker-owned enterprises in Canada that have been planned without an external "parent." For example, CRS[37] -- a worker co-operative in Vancouver -- is reputed to be the largest wholesaler of natural foods in Western Canada. It has been able to provide good earnings and quality working conditions for its members. Another interesting example is the Big Carrot natural food market in Toronto.[38] Started originally by nine unemployed workers, it quickly took off as a business and has recently undertaken a major expansion to a 7,000-square-foot (super)market located in a 14-store mall called Carrot Common in which the Big Carrot holds a 35 per cent interest.

When one studies these exceptions, the image of the guiding parent often emerges. The parent is, however, a member of the business who assumes a leadership role in business planning. Rather than applying their energies to creating their own business, these exceptional individuals prefer to function in a collective context. For want of a better term, we might refer to this motivation as the "Robert Owen syndrome" -- after the nineteenth century British industrialist who participated in planning the model community and cotton mill at New Lanark, Scotland, and whose ideas inspired the first experiment in worker ownership at Rochdale, England.[39]

Harpell Printing of Montréal, a 165-member worker-owned business, was created in 1945 when the owner of a privately-owned printing business, James-John Harpell, decided that he wanted to sell it to the workers.[40] His motivation was social. Like Robert Owen, he wanted to demonstrate that society could be changed. Similarly, much of the success of the Big Carrot is because of the leadership provided by Mary Lou Morgan, a woman with much experience in the natural food business and with obvious entrepreneurial talents, and because of the financing of Carrot Common by David Walsh, a real-estate developer who is involved in the Catholic social-justice movement.[41] Walsh arranged for the $6.5 million financial package and granted 35 per cent of the equity to the Big Carrot and 15 per cent to other community-based groups.

Attributing the success of worker co-operatives to one or two leaders does not do justice to the contribution of all its worker-owners or outside consultants who have assisted in various ways. However, there are paradoxes about the worker-ownership model that, unless understood and dealt with constructively, will impede development. Worker-owned enterprises, like businesses in general, function in a competitive market that demands certain adaptive qualities. In conventionally-owned businesses, these qualities are provided by the owners and senior management, who provide organization and direction. The workers serve as employees under the guidance of senior management. By contrast, in worker-owned businesses, the members have dual functions of worker and owner. They are not only guided but also provide guidance -- either directly or indirectly through the appointment of management.

Unfortunately, public education in Canada (and many other countries) does not encourage the combination of characteristics required of worker-owners. People who are inclined toward business ownership usually thrive on risks but expect to exert control. Entrepreneurs are unlikely to share control with a group, particularly if the members lack entrepreneurial skills and capital.

Worker-owned enterprises must cope with the paradox that, in order to succeed, they require some members who have entrepreneurial and management qualities but who have the same ownership rights as other workers without these qualities. Ideally, a worker co-operative has an educational program which assists all members to participate in aspects of management and business planning. However, there are practical limitations such as cost, time, and talent which work against a broad distribution of entrepreneurial skills -- limitations which become greater as a co-operative increases in size. Inevitably, there must be some recruitment of experienced entrepreneurs, and inevitably the one-member/one-vote feature of a worker co-operative is a disincentive for such individuals.

The structure of worker-owned enterprises presents other problems. It means that unless the business involves people of similar skills, there will be a large disparity in the earnings of members. In theory, paying members according to the market value of their job should be possible and is done. However, if the market value leads to differences that are too extreme, social problems may result. The Mondragon co-ops have experienced tension because senior management has pushed to have its pay increased from the traditional ratio of three times the lowest-paid job to the market rate for similar jobs in private industry.[42] Consequently, unless their salaries are increased, senior management may leave for better paid jobs. Again, the egalitarian structure of worker-owned enterprises acts as a disincentive for a broad division of labour as is found in other modern businesses.

There is another handicap associated with the worker-ownership structure. As owners, workers are expected to capitalize their business. The egalitarian structure means that the financial resources of the "average" worker-member will become the norm. Because these resources are not large, there is a tendency for worker-owned enterprises to be poorly financed and labour intensive. Virtually all worker-owned enterprises in Canada are comprised of members with similar skills and with limited finances. These businesses have attracted very few professionals and persons with managerial training.

When one also considers that worker co-operatives operate independently without proper support systems, it is understandable that development remains weak. The situation of worker-owned enterprises in Canada is analogous to small boats with minimally-trained crews trying to make their way through a stormy sea. The journey, though exciting, can be quite perilous.

The pattern of worker co-operative development in Canada is a direct result of tendencies within the structure of these enterprises interacting with a competitive market that plays havoc with all enterprises. The existing pattern is apparent; less obvious is how to change it.

A Development Model for Canada

The key elements in a development plan are the need for a system that provides sources for entrepreneurship and capital and which also provides ongoing support for co-operative enterprises so that in a competitive market they can enjoy the same advantages as privately-owned enterprises.

Co-operative Entrepreneurship

Where a system of worker-owned enterprises already exists, it becomes the source of entrepreneurial talent. In Mondragon, for example, entrepreneurship is fostered by assisting members of existing co-ops to develop business ideas that can form the basis for new co-ops. Those members then become the leadership group for the new enterprise and work with the Caja's consultants to assess the feasibility and to do the organizational planning.[43] Their reward comes from seeing their idea realized and their promotion to managerial roles within the new enterprise. PACE has adopted this approach on a smaller scale. Managers for new supermarkets are drawn from talented persons in existing ones.[44]

Developing entrepreneurial talent becomes a more formidable problem when such a system does not exist. As noted, the void is filled to a degree by atypical individuals with entrepreneurial skills who are either members of worker co-operatives or consultants with resource groups. At present, there are too few of these persons for significant development to occur. Furthermore, without a reasonable source of income, co-operative entrepreneurs will find other causes.

In Québec, co-operative entrepreneurs have been drawn to the development of worker co-operatives by government financing.[45] Thus, persons with entrepreneurial talents have joined development groups (groupe conseils) where they receive salaries derived from government grants. In addition, persons with entrepreneurial talents have been drawn to worker co-ops because of financing for development available through the Société de développement des coopératives (a government agency).[46] Neither financing for development groups nor financing on the same scale for worker co-operatives is available in other parts of Canada. Without these important incentives for institutionalizing an ongoing source of entrepreneurship, worker co-operative development outside of Québec has been sporadic. And even in Québec, the approach to development is primarily reactive, though recently change has been occurring. The forestry co-operatives, the major worker-owned enterprises in the province, have formed federations (both general and regional), have developed a specialized resource group, and have achieved a scale that has necessitated the involvement of professionals in management and planning. Like Mondragon, Québec's forestry co-operatives are gradually institutionalizing a source of entrepreneurship.

These recent changes in the forestry sector are reflective of a gradual shift within Québec toward a more proactive approach to planning. The Montréal-Laval resource group, for example, has picked up an approach pioneered in France called Campus Co-operatives that involves bringing together teams of entrepreneurs who, together with the resource group, plan a worker-owned enterprise.[47] This same shift is occuring in Britain, where recently at least two British development groups -- the Scottish Co-operative Development Committee (SCDC) and the Cleveland Development Association -- have departed from tradition and have adopted features of the Mondragon approach to encourage entrepreneurship.[48] In those cases, the development group identifies market niches, undertakes preliminary feasibility analyses, and advertises for "co-operative entrepreneurs." These persons then work with a consultant from the development group to initiate the business plan and to put together the co-operative. As an incentive for accepting this role, the "co-operative entrepreneur" is put on salary for up to six months.

There's a risk in this approach because the co-operative entrepreneur who takes the lead in the initial planning may retain a privileged status within the co-operative, a role that might eventually prove incompatible with the egalitarian values of the enterprise. This risk must be balanced against the benefits of having sound planning and well-prepared management. The SCDC and Cleveland adaptations of Mondragon assure that planning expertise essential to the success of the business is not only lodged in the development group (as in Québec's groupe-conseils or other British development groups) but also becomes part of the co-operative from the very beginning.

To implement this practice, government funding (i.e., job-training money) and a method of recruitment are required. Both of these requirements should be realizable in Canada although, judging by the British experience, recruitment of co-operative entrepreneurs could prove the greater difficulty. A method for overcoming this problem might be to establish programs on co-operative entrepreneurship in community colleges or to actively recruit from other social movements.[49]

System Building

The problems of co-operative entrepreneurship and financing are best dealt with through a system of co-operatives.[50] There are formidable obstacles to system building in Canada, including the tradition of independence among worker co-operatives, strong regional loyalties buffered by vast distances, low population densities, and cultural and linguistic pluralities. The Evangeline group is an excellent example of a system, but it has evolved in a tightly knit Acadian community which is atypical of modern societies.[51] Where strong community ties do exist (primarily in rural areas), it seems appropriate to envision worker co-operatives as part of a system of co-operatives of all types -- such as Evangeline.[52] The difficulty here (as has been noted by George Melnyk) is that co-operative tradition has been "unifunctional,"[53] insofar as each co-operative relates to superordinate organizations within its own sector and only peripherally to other sectors. There are indications though that the credit-union movement is encouraging community development.[54] Where communities actually exist, a strong educational campaign, reinforced by models such as Evangeline, could move development in that direction. The advantage of building systems of all forms of co-operatives (not just worker co-operatives) is that the credit unions in the system can organize the financial package. Also, there is federal-government money available for industrial development in rural areas that can lead

to better financing than is usually available for worker
co-operatives.

Within urban contexts, the key to building a system of
unifunctional co-operatives (including worker co-operatives)
comes from the housing sector.[55] By its very nature, a housing
co-operative is a type of community. Unlike a credit union, for
example, a housing co-operative represents a major part of a
member's lifespace and is important to his/her identity. As a
relatively young movement, the housing sector has an idealistic
leadership that is encouraging an interest in other forms of
co-operatives. Not surprisingly then, a number of housing
co-operatives in Canada have assisted the formation of worker
and consumer co-operatives that provide additional services to
their members.[56]

In spite of some potential, building a system of co-operatives
around a geographic community like a housing co-operative is not
likely to have a major impact upon worker co-operative
development. In the average housing co-op there is insufficient
interest in other co-operative organizations for there to be any
extensive development of urban clusters. The idea, though, could
be experimented with through a pilot project, and if successful,
might spread.

Adapting the PACE Approach

For urban parts of Canada, the developmental model created
by PACE appears to be practical. As noted, PACE's approach has
been to create a system around a specific industry. PACE's
founder and director, Sherman Kreiner, refers to this approach as
"targeting."[57] Identifying markets for worker co-operatives in
Canada and building systems around them is a logical extension
of the PACE approach. Essentially, the development group
becomes the nucleus of a cell that includes a set of worker-owned
enterprises tied by a common sector of the market. Because of
the similarity of the enterprises, development costs are reduced.

Regionalism would probably place constraints on the work of
a market-specific development group. It is difficult to foresee that
a development group specializing in forestry and located in
Ontario, for example, would be readily accepted in British

Columbia. Therefore, development groups might create market-specific systems within regions, and then, perhaps, exchange market expertise with development groups in other regions.[58]

At present, the general orientation of the worker co-operative movement in English Canada is to create "five regionally-based enterprise centres" to provide assistance as requested.[59] The Canadian Co-operative Association is lobbying the federal government to underwrite the cost of such a proposal. Assuming success, this proposal would increase the number of qualified business consultants in the field -- an important step forward -- but without a proactive, system-building approach the current problems of high failure rates and a lack of business development are unlikely to change.

To overcome these same problems the conventional business community has created franchises. This arrangement is incompatible with the worker co-operative because it denies the members of each individual enterprise some rights of corporate control. However, as demonstrated by PACE, it is possible to utilize some aspects of the franchise through the creation of a system of worker co-operatives in which the members of an individual enterprise have collective control over their own co-operative, and those same co-operatives have links with each other through the development group that planned them and through a second-tier co-operative that does purchasing and marketing.

There appears to be two practical difficulties in combining the regional enterprise approach with the building of a system of market-specific worker co-operatives. If there is only one "enterprise centre" in a region, worker co-operatives of all types would turn to it for services, and the enterprise centre would therefore want to retain enough general expertise to deal with these requests. One solution to this difficulty would be for enterprise centres to provide both a general consulting service and a proactive planning strategy for specific markets. It might also be advisable for consultants in enterprise centres to look more critically at independent initiatives and to make prospective members aware of the track record of such initiatives.

A second practical difficulty to this approach is arranging proper financing for prospective enterprises. Unlike Mondragon where the development group is a division of a credit co-operative, the PACE adaptation requires arranging a variety of sources for the financial package of each project. PACE's director, Sherman Kreiner, argues that something similar to the Caja is needed in North America.[60] Kreiner outlines two possibilities: either a credit co-operative like Mondragon or a ventures fund like the Québec Federation of Labour Solidarity Fund. The Scottish worker co-operative movement has chosen the ventures approach. With the support of organized labour, the ventures approach could be appropriate for Canada.

If it could be organized, a depositor-based credit co-operative has a distinct advantage. The revenues from developing co-operatives are channeled into the corporation that is financing them, thereby enhancing the financing for new enterprises. The words 'if it could be organized' are not to be trivialized; nor is the oft-stated criticism that the credit co-operative as in Mondragon has a great deal of control. The greatest check against abuse, Kreiner argues, is for the financial organization to be structured as a second-tier co-operative whose members are the businesses which are being created. Even if the member co-ops do not deal with technical policy, they would have corporate control, including the right to appoint senior management. Though not a guarantee against abuse, this power is an important check.

One additional observation might be made about the PACE approach. In proposing its utilization in Canada I have referred to regional barriers. Given that this paper is conceptual, I might allude to the inconceivable and think about Canada-United States collaboration both for building systems of worker co-operatives in a market sector and for establishing a credit co-operative. PACE has established expertise in the food sector, so it would make sense to utilize that expertise in Canada and similarly for specialized development groups in Canada to extend their system-building techniques to the United States. Also, the scope of a credit co-operative could be enhanced if the depositors and the member co-operatives were from Canada and the United States.

Multi-Stakeholder Systems

Another possibility for system-building that could overcome the problem of capitalization would be to link worker ownership to an existing organization with a solid financial base. An example of such an approach is the multi-stakeholder co-operative described by John Jordan (see Chapter 5). The Co-operators' Group, the holding company for Co-operators Insurance (Canada's largest general insurance company) and seven other subsidiaries, is converting its associated enterprises to a multi-stakeholder model that includes the workers as one stakeholder of the control structure;[61] the others are consumers of each subsidiary's service and the Group itself, which provides much of the capital. The Co-operators has now established this model in three subsidiaries, and assuming positive results, it is anticipated that the model will be extended to others.

Like the other approaches to system-building, there are advantages and disadvantages. A major advantage is that each subsidiary is properly capitalized and embedded in a system anchored by a major corporation. The workers' investment is much less at risk than in a small, isolated enterprise. The importance of this consideration should not be underestimated. Moreover, by starting with either an existing enterprise with established markets or new enterprises sheltered within a corporate system, a major problem for isolated starts (namely, establishing a market presence) is lessened. Although the Co-operators' multi-stakeholders have to develop their markets, they start with a solid financial base and a credible reputation. They also embody a broader range of job skills, including more professionals, than most worker co-operatives. Arguably, having this range is better for the company's future, although this point is open to conjecture.

The disadvantage of the multi-stakeholder model is that the workers have less control at the board level than in a worker co-operative. This means that the members of the enterprise might face board decisions with which they disagree, including a decision to dissolve or sell the business. In the case of the Co-operators which is owned by other co-operatives, a sale for a quick profit is unlikely. There is also a philosophical argument to be made in favour of the multi-stakeholder control structure. It balances consumers' interests with workers' interests. Arguably, this overcomes a weakness of the worker co-operative which (like some privately-owned businesses) could enter into an exploitive relationship with the consumer.

There have been some other experiments with a multi-stakeholder arrangement in Canada. North Lake Fishermen's Co-op was formed recently from the United Maritime Fishermen's Co-op that went bankrupt.[62] The stakeholders are fish catchers and plant workers. Similar arrangements apply to other fishery co-operatives, including Fogo Island and Torngat of Newfoundland.[63] These fishery co-operatives, however, bear the risks of isolated enterprises functioning without a system. Moreover, plant workers are usually included in the co-operative as a method of increasing financing.

Although the multi-stakeholder model has been applied in Canada within the co-operative corporation, it could be organized in other systems, for example, organized labour. In Israel, for example, Argaz, a worker co-operative that manufactures furniture and assembles buses, is half-owned by the Histradut, the central labour federation.[64] This came about when Argaz was unable to take in new members because its share value of $25,000 (U.S.) was beyond the financial reach of its 850 hired workers. Argaz's 150 members were aging and retiring, thereby draining the company of capital. To prevent the company from being sold into private hands, as had happened with other Israeli co-operatives in similar circumstances, the Histradut took a 50 per cent financial stake.

The Histradut, unlike organized labour in Canada, owns a substantial part of the Israeli economy through the Chevrat Ovdim (the Association of Workers). Thus Argaz, through the Histradut's stake, has been drawn into a system. (In theory it was already part of the system because members of Israeli worker co-operatives also belong to the central labour federation.) There are features of the Argaz example that are less than desirable, particularly the large number of hired workers. Nevertheless, Argaz illustrates that a multi-stakeholder system can be introduced not only with an umbrella co-operative but also with organized labour.

In Canada, organized labour has not been inclined to become a "major" stakeholder of either privately-owned companies or co-operatives. Labour-controlled venture capital funds (e.g., Québec's Solidarity Fund)[65] make only a small investment in any particular business, including worker co-operatives.[66] And like organized labour, the co-operative sector has not as yet shown any general desire to shift from a unifunctional to multi-stakeholder approach. The results of the Co-operators' experiment still are incomplete.

Conclusion

Although there have been some very successful developments, worker co-operatives in Canada have suffered from problems that afflict small businesses in general. Undercapitalization, weak marketing, a lack of careful planning, and the isolation of each enterprise have resulted in high failure rates and low earnings.

In this chapter, I proposed that these problems could be addressed by a proactive approach to development whereby professional planners in development groups identify markets for prospective enterprises and, in partnership with co-operative entrepreneurs, carefully plan the start of a new business. I also proposed that the stability of worker co-operatives would be enhanced by building systems of companies rather than concentrating on isolated enterprises.

Three types of systems were outlined. First, there could be clusters of co-operatives in which worker co-operatives would be one component of a group that served a community's needs. The Evangeline group in the Acadian section of Prince Edward Island is an example of such a cluster. In rural communities, where this model would seem most applicable, it is anticipated that the credit union would be the hub of the cluster. In urban areas where the prospects for this approach are not as good, housing co-operatives might form the hub.

Second, there could be systems of worker co-operatives both within a market sector and within a region. The development group would initially be the hub of the system, though the central role would eventually pass to a second-tier co-operative of which each worker co-operative was a member. Financing would be arranged from available sources. Ideally, however, this approach should include a credit co-operative as in Mondragon. The best example of this approach in North America is PACE of Philadelphia, which has specialized in creating a system of (O&O stores) worker-owned supermarkets.

Finally, it would be possible to create a group of multi-stakeholder co-operatives that was either related to or subsidiary to an established co-operative. In Canada, the Co-operators Group is currently creating such a system. In theory it is possible to create a multi-stakeholder system with organized labour, although organized labour in Canada has shown no interest in doing this.

Each of these three approaches to system building is conceptual, but each is based on at least one existing experiment which suggests that the approach is workable. Even though these three approaches differ, use of one does not preclude use of another. Rather than dwell on one single approach, it seems important to recognize the common feature of integrating individual worker co-operatives into a more robust system that can cope with a dynamic marketplace. The argument in favour of a system is based in part upon its success where tried and the recognition that experiments in creating independent worker co-operatives over the past 100 years have not been overly successful.[67]

The evidence suggests that small independent enterprises, financed and developed by groups of workers, create primarily a type of business counterculture, which may have meaning to the individuals involved, but is unlikely to have any significant or enduring impact on the economy. Unless the members do not care about survival and view the creation of the co-operative as a transient learning experience, they must be advised that the risks -- as for small independent businesses in general -- are very high and that the prospects for success are greatly enhanced through involvement in a system. The three approaches to system building presented in this chapter do not exhaust the possibilities. They are, however, illustrative of the possibilities.

Notes

[1] Worker co-operatives and worker-owned enterprises are used interchangeably throughout this chapter.

[2] Johanne Berard, "Fifty Years of Worker Co-operatives in Québec, *Worker Co-op*, 7, No. 1 (1987), 10-12.

[3] Chris Cornforth, "The Effectiveness of British Support Organizations in Developing Worker Co-operatives," *Worker Co-op*, 6, No.2 (1986), 11.

[4] Keith Jeffries, "A Profile of ICOM Co-ops," *Worker Co-op*, 6, No. 3 (1987), 34.

[5] Jacques LaRue, "Why Québec Is so Successful in Developing Worker Co-co-operatives," *Worker Co-op*, 6, No.2 (1987), 42-43.

[6] Jack Quarter, "The Middlesbrough Initiative," *Worker Co-op*, 8, No. 2 (1988), 36.

[7] "Mondragon Co-ops Continue their Remarkable Growth," *Worker Co-op*, 8, No. 1 (1988), 38-39.

[8] Russell Christianson, "Mondragon," *Worker Co-op*, 7, No. 1 (1987), 21-22.

[9] Chris Axworthy, *Worker Co-operatives in Mondragon, the U.K. and France: Some Reflections* (Saskatoon, Sask.: Centre for the Study of Co-operatives, 1985), 1-20.

[10] Alain Roy, *Worker Co-operatives: The Canadian Scene* (Ottawa: Co-op Secretariat, June 1988), 22 pp.

[11] A problem in providing a precise profile of worker co-operatives in Canada is that Statistics Canada figures are two years out of date and based on the type of incorporation (i.e., co-operative corporation) rather than the organizational characteristics. Some enterprises which are incorporated as limited companies or partnerships have the organizational structure of a worker co-operative. The estimates in this chapter are pieced together from both Statistics Canada and from more up-to-date regional reports in *Worker Co-op*.

[12] Maureen Coady, "Unprecedented Growth for Nova Scotia Worker Co-ops," *Worker Co-op*, 8, No. 1 (1988), 16.

[13] Alain Côté, "Ten Thousand Québec Workers Try Another Way," *Worker Co-op*, 6, No. 1 (1986), 8-9.

[14] Claude Carbonneau, "Forestry Co-ops Ring up $180 Million in Sales," *Worker Co-op*, 8, No. 1 (1988), 14.

[15]John Jordan, "Developing Worker Co-operatives" *Co-operative College of Canada Working Papers*, 2, No. 6 (1984), 1-44.

[16]Côté, "Ten thousand Québec Workers," pp. 8-9.

[17]Udo Staber, "Survival Rates for Maritime Worker Co-ops," *Worker Co-op*, 8, No. 1 (1988), 36-37.

[18]Roy, "The Canadian Scene," p. 17.

[19]The more rapid failure rate for Québec worker co-ops may reflect either regional differences or procedural differences. The latter seems more likely. The Québec data are based on a co-op remaining active; the Maritime data seem to be less precise about inactivity and rely more on cancellation of the incorporation.

[20]Christianson, "Mondragon," pp. 21-22.

[21]Lankide Aurrezkia, *The Mondragon Experiment* (Mondragon: Caja Laboral Popular, 1984).

[22]"Mondragon: Employment," *Worker Co-op*, 7, No. 2 (1987), 25.

[23]Robert Oakeshott, *The Case for Workers' Co-ops* (London: Routledge & Kegan Paul, 1978), Chapter 10.

[24]Jack Quarter, "Senior Management Leaving as Mondragon Faces New Challenges," *Worker Co-op*, 6, No. 2 (1986), 19-20.

[25]Anna Gutierrez Johnson and William Foote Whyte, "The Mondragon System of Production Co-operatives," in *Workplace Democracy and Social Change*, ed. Frank Lindenfeld and Joyce Rothschild-Whitt (Boston: Porter-Sargent, 1982), p. 188.

[26]For a more recent discussion see W.F. Whyte and K.K. Whyte, *Making Mondragon* (New York: Cornell University Press, 1988).

[27]Chris Axworthy, "Some Cons about Mondragon," *Worker Co-op*, 5, No. 2 (1985), 21-22.

[28]Sherman Kreiner, "Unions and Worker Ownership: Traditional and Emerging Roles," *Worker Co-op*, 5, No. 4 (1986), 12-15.

[29]Cynthia Coker and Virginia Vanderslice, "The PACE Worker-Education Program," *Worker Co-op*, 7, No. 1 (1987), 15-16.

[30]"Mondragon: Canadian Products in Demand," *Worker Co-op*, 7, No. 4 (1988), 32.

[31]Sherman Kreiner, "A Targeted Approach to Worker Co-operative Development in North America," *Worker Co-op*, 8, No. 2 (1988), 19-21.

[32]Dennis Clark and Merry Guben, *Future Bread* (Philadelphia: O&O Investment Fund, 1984).

[33]Personal Communication.

[34]Emile Gallant, "P.E.I. Potato Chip Co-op Is a Community Effort," *Worker Co-op*, 6, No. 2 (1986), 36-37.

[35]Brian Iler, "P.E.I. Potato-Chip Co-op," *Worker Co-op*, 7, No. 3 (1988), 14.

[36]Raymond Arsenault, "Evangeline, Prince Edward Island, the Uncontested Co-op Capital," *Worker Co-op*, 7, No. 3 (1988), 7-10.

[37]Melanie Conn and Dana Weber, "CRS May Be Number One in Western Canada," *Worker Co-op*, 7, No. 3 (1988), 36-37.

[38]Jack Quarter, "Mary Lou Morgan Dreams and The Big Carrot Grows," *Worker Co-op*, 7, No. 2 (1987), 22-24.

[39]Oakeshott, *The Case for Workers' Co-ops*, pp. 55-56.

[40]Paul Vincent, "James-John Harpell: Pioneer of Worker Co-ops in Canada," *Worker Co-op*, 6, No. 4 (1987), 11-12.

[41]Quarter, "Mary Lou Morgan Dreams," pp. 22-24.

[42]Quarter, "Senior Management Leaving," pp. 19-20.

[43]Oakeshott, *The Case for Workers' Co-ops*, Chapter 10.

[44]Kreiner, "A Targeted Approach," pp. 19-21.

[45]Claude Carbonneau, "Feds Cough Up $1.6 Million for Québec Development Groups," *Worker Co-op*, 8, No. 1 (1988), 13-14.

[46]Claude Carbonneau, "Increased Role for S.D.C.," *Worker Co-op*, 7, No. 1 (1987), 31.

[47]Luc Labelle, "Montréal Resource Group Launches Innovative Approach to Development," *Worker Co-op*, 8, No. 3 (1989), 15-17.

[48]Jack Quarter, "Wanted: Co-operative Entrepreneurs," *Worker Co-op*, 8, No. 2 (1988) 36.

[49]Cornforth, "The Effectiveness of British Support Organizations," p. 11.

[50]Jordan, "Developing Worker Co-operatives."

[51]Arsenault, "Evangeline, Prince Edward Island, the Uncontested Co-op Capital," pp. 7-10.

[52]Jack Quarter, "Building Communities of Co-operatives," Paper Presented at the Conference of the International Association of Communal Studies, New Lanark, Scotland, July 1988.

[53]George Melnyk, *The Search for Community* (Montréal: Black Rose, 1985), Chapter 2.

[54]The Canadian Co-operative Credit Society (CCCS), the national organization for Canadian credit unions, has created an annual award for the credit union which does the most for economic development in its community.

[55]Quarter, "Building Communities of Co-operatives."

[56]Dana Weber, "Housing Co-ops Learn about Worker Co-ops," *Worker Co-op*, 8, No. 1 (1988), 9.

[57]Kreiner, "A Targeted Approach," pp. 19-21.

[58]For an interesting discussion of a regional approach see: J. T. Webb, *Workers' Co-operatives: A People-Centred Approach to Regional Development* (Moncton: Institut Canadien de Resherche sur le Développement Regional, 1987), 200 pp.

[59]Albert Chambers, "CCA Makes Worker Co-ops an Election Priority," *Worker Co-op*, 8, No. 2 (1988), 24.

[60]Kreiner, "A Targeted Approach," pp. 19-21.

[61]Teunis Haalboom and John Jordan, "The Multi-Stakeholder Co-operative," *Worker Co-op*, 6, No. 3 (1987), 10-14.

[62]Frank Driscoll, "The Phoenix Rises from UMF's Ashes," *Worker Co-op*, 8, No. 1 (1988), 19.

[63]Robert Thompson, "Regional Profile: Newfoundland and Labrador," *Worker Co-op*, 5, No. 1 (1985), 8.

[64]Jack Quarter, "Worker co-operatives in Israel: The Complex Relationship with Organized Labour," *Worker Co-op*, 5, No. 2 (1985), 17-18.

[65]Albert Chambers, "February 1988 Budget," *Worker Co-op*, 7, No. 4 (1988), 18.

[66]Claude Carbonneau, "Federation of Worker Co-operatives," *Worker Co-op*, 7, No. 4 (1988), 21-22.

[67]Ian MacPherson, "Reflections on the Uneven History of Worker Co-operatives in Canada," *Worker Co-op*, 6, No. 4 (1987), 8-10.

Chapter 3

From Worker Buyouts to a Conversions Strategy

Jack Quarter and Jo-Ann Hannah

There are only a smattering of successful worker buyouts across Canada. In this chapter we will present some case studies that pinpoint the basic problems in workers buying companies that are under a threat of closure. Although selected worker buyouts can succeed with early detection and appropriate supports, we propose that it would be more effective to develop a conversions strategy that encourages employees to purchase their place of work when it is healthy rather than at the brink of collapse.

Lamford Forest Products[1]

"The mill with 250 bosses" is the way that the *Report on Business*[2] magazine described the Lamford buyout. With sales for 1987 projected at $45 million, the Lamford buyout has involved both sound planning and fortuitous circumstances and is the cause célèbre of the worker-ownership movement. Unlike many other closings, the shutdown of Lamford's predecessor, Sooke Forest Products, was not planned by its owners; that is, the owners did not permit their plants to become run down prior to closure. Rather, they invested heavily in modernizing the company's two mills at Westminister and at Sooke, Vancouver Island, as part of a plan to make the business successful. Circumstances conspired against them: Their debt was a massive $55.8 million, interest rates unexpectedly spiraled to 22 per cent, and the price for forest products declined. The decision to close was made not by the owners, as is usually the case with plant closures, but by their creditors.

In July 1984, the Toronto Dominion Bank began foreclosing procedures against the two mills because revenues could no longer service the debt. Even though the mills at Sooke and Westminister were in excellent condition with an estimated market value of close to $20 million, the British Columbia forestry industry was in a slump (eight publicly-traded companies had posted after-tax losses of $456 million) and buyers were not lining up. Given the quality of the mills, this was unusual but fortunate for the workers.

Two Vancouver entrepreneurs did come forward with a proposal that involved the workers putting up all of the necessary cash in exchange for 38 per cent of the voting stock. The workers did not bite, but this offer spurred union and senior management to get together and to prepare their own offer. The initiative came from the senior managers of the two mills (Bob Anderson and Don McMillan), the leaders of Locals 1-357 and 1-118 of the International Woodworkers Association (Terry Smith and Roger Lewis), the union accountant (David Korbin), and the lawyer (Roger Lewis).

Although the IWA was supportive of the Lamford buyout, this commitment was based on circumstance rather than principle. A year earlier, when workers at another British Columbia plant, Pacific Forest Products, purchased the business and established it as a worker co-operative (Victoria Plywood), the IWA did not support the buyout because a condition of obtaining financing was a substantial reduction in wages.[3] Also, unlike Sooke, the equipment at Pacific Forest Products was in need of a major modernization.

Terry Smith, president of Local 1-357 of the IWA, is very clear about these points:

Victoria Plywood was a very outmoded plant, a difficult plant
to operate, and one that was losing horrendous amounts of
money. A group of people thought they could put it together
under a co-operative structure, but only if they took very
significant wage cuts that could affect unionized plants
elsewhere. If you work for $8 an hour, as against $15 an hour
in an unionized plant, obviously you should be successful if you
sell your plywood at the prices unionized mills are getting.

Despite our involvement in Lamford, I don't think you can say
that IWA has become an absolute supporter of worker
ownership. We are not going to get involved in worker buyouts
every time a plant closure comes along . . . . Lamford was a
unique situation, and it was not one that required a direct
financial commitment from the union.[4]

With senior management and union working in concert and
the workers without other opportunities in a recession-hit
industry, the circumstances were favourable for a worker buyout.
However, the price also had to be affordable, and in this respect
the workers were fortunate. Nearly a year after closing, there
were no prospective buyers, so the TD Bank lowered its asking
price. The workers were able to purchase the inventory, plant,
and equipment for $3 million, carried by the bank in the form of a
loan at seven per cent. In exchange, the union waived
proceedings to recover severance pay, and Lamford agreed to
disencumber property taxes owed by Sooke. With working capital
requirements for the new organization, the total financial
package was estimated at about $14 million.

As with most worker buyouts, arranging the financing was
not simple. The Bank of British Columbia agreed to a credit line
for operating capital of $6 million on condition that the workers
come up with $2.5 million. A $500,000 loan from the CCEC credit
union, of which Smith was a Board member, started the process,
and the workers were able to obtain the remaining $2 million
from the B.C. Development Corporation, a provincial Crown
corporation. Each worker holds $12,500 worth of Class B shares
to be paid through a 17 per cent payroll deduction. In addition,
each worker holds a common or voting share.

Lamford is incorporated as a limited company, as are many
other worker-owned corporations. The Board consists of three
outside directors, presidents of the two union locals involved, two

representatives of salaried workers, and two representatives of hourly-paid workers.

It took until January 1986, before the two mills were back in operation. By then, the industry had recovered, and Lamford's 1986 sales were double those of Sooke during its final year. The workers inherited a company with a good name, with modern equipment, and at a price that was a steal. The story continues, as with all businesses. A recent downturn in the forest industry has caused some financial strain and layoffs at Lamford.[5] That notwithstanding, the Lamford story is still a happy one. The company recently received the Canada Award for Business Excellence in Labour-Management Co-operation,[6] and Lamford's success has been widely publicized in the media.

Canadian Porcelain[7]

The circumstances that helped make the Lamford buyout successful were not typical. Events surrounding the closure of Canadian Porcelain provide more insight into why a worker buyout is so difficult to organize. Although workersat Canadian Porcelain were determined to buy the plant and had substantial support from the community, their efforts failed.

Canadian Porcelain was a Hamilton plant which manufactured electrical porcelain insulators. At the time of closing in December 1984, it was Canada's only major manufacturer of this product, even though the domestic market was about $20 million annually. Canadian Porcelain had operated successfully in Hamilton since 1912, servicing both domestic and foreign markets. Initially a family business, from 1958 to closing it went through a series of ownership changes which, with the exception of its last three years, involved being a subsidiary of American corporations. There were several consequences to these ownership changes: access to the company's foreign markets were denied, profits were siphoned off, equipment was not modernized, and the workforce was slashed in half from its peak of 140 workers.

When the economy slumped in 1982, sales at Canadian

Porcelain fell sharply. Foreign competitors also had to cope with a slumping market and began dumping porcelain insulators onto the Canadian market (something for which they were convicted by an Anti-Dumping Tribunal). In December 1984, the Royal Bank placed Canadian Porcelain into receivership. To that point, the Canadian Porcelain drama was not unlike many other plant closings played out across Canada; but with Canadian Porcelain, the circumstances following the closing were somewhat unusual. Hamilton had been hit hard by plant closings, and as a result, community leaders rallied about the plant, determined to find a way of keeping it open.

An organization called the Christians for a Co-operative Society, led by church leaders, made a public issue out of reviving the plant. Together with the leadership from Local 249 of the Aluminum, Brick & Glass Workers Union, they interested the workers in a buyout. Doing so was not a simple matter. The workers showed little initial interest, but with the union's leadership and the support of community groups, a worker co-operative consisting of 60 of Canadian Porcelain's workers was incorporated. The President was Bill Thompson, secretary of the union local.

The commitment to incorporate the co-operative, albeit important, did not cost the workers anything. The difficult step was arranging financing to purchase the company from the receiver, Peat Marwick. Like most workers, those at Canadian Porcelain lacked cash for the $1.5 million asking price. In order to obtain loans, it was necessary to have a feasibility study demonstrating that the business could operate successfully. Even the feasibility study required money which the workers lacked, but it was eventually paid for by the provincial and municipal governments.

The first feasibility analysis by a large accountancy firm was very negative. A subsequent feasibility study by Co-operative Work, at that time a Toronto consulting group specializing in business planning for worker co-operatives, was positive because it took into account the effect of a new tariff to protect the industry. With the positive feasibility in hand, the worker co-operative was able to put together a financial offer of $1.1

million, backed by the Hamilton-Wentworth credit union (which made $5,000 loans available to each worker), the Ontario Credit Union Central, and CUMIS and The Co-operators insurance companies. Again, arranging the financing was difficult, and it probably would not have been possible had there not been such strong community support for the buyout.

Just when negotiations between the worker co-operative and the receiver were proceeding, a bid of $1.25 million was tendered by Lapp Insulators of New York, one of the companies which had been convicted of dumping. This bid was accepted without offering the worker co-operative an opportunity to exceed it. The receiver's decision to sell the Hamilton plant to Lapp was appealed without success to the federal cabinet. The worker co-operative and its supporters argued that Lapp, in spite of its many promises, had no serious commitment to the Hamilton plant. It simply did not want a competitor there.

Sinclair Stevens, the minister responsible, lacked confidence in the workers' offer. Stevens was quoted as saying:

> We could not convince ourselves that if we said no to the American proposal, the Canadian workers could indeed purchase the assets and set up what they were hoping to set up.[8]

History, for what it was worth, proved the workers' view to be accurate. Just two years after purchasing the Hamilton plant, Lapp decided to close it.[9] Lapp has the Québec market and is asking $10 million for the plant[10] ($9 million more than it paid two years earlier). THe workers are without their jobs, and the co-operative remains a dream. It is also noteworthy that the free-trade agreement between Canada and the United States will remove the protective tariff upon which the co-operative's business plan was predicated.

The Beef Terminal[11]

In June 1979, Junction Holdings closed the second largest packinghouse in Ontario -- the Beef Terminal. By October of that year, an employee group led by the general manager and other management personnel had purchased the company. The period during which the Beef Terminal shut down was difficult for the packinghouse industry. Nine packinghouses were closed between 1978 and 1979, and there were no buyers for the Beef Terminal prior to the 1979 closing.

The original business was a "comprehensive" packinghouse with sales in excess of $75 million. About 2,500 head of cattle were purchased each week at stockyards throughout Canada and were slaughtered on the Beef Terminal's kill-floor. The product was later sold to customers, including all of the food chains in Ontario.

The general manager of the business, Jim Wilson, determined that the major problem with the packinghouse was the large cash outlay to purchase cattle and a lengthy delay before payments were received from customers -- a problem that became more acute as interest rates increased. He was convinced that the business could be successful if it were limited to the slaughterhouse; that is, customers would purchase their own animals and bring them to the Beef Terminal for slaughter. Payments at a price per head would be made within a week.

Wilson, who undertook this feasibility analysis, convinced a group of nine staff (most of them managers of the former operation) that his business plan would work. But the group lacked the financing to purchase the kill-floor and its equipment (valued at $5 million). Rather than a straight purchase, it was decided to lease the slaughterhouse with an option to purchase within three years. This arrangement was agreeable to Junction Holdings because it lacked other buyers, and the possibility of a purchase was preferable to liquidation.

The purchasing group of nine still needed additional financing. Government assistance was refused, and lending institutions wanted a sizeable investment before making a loan. Therefore, the group of nine selected 31 former employees, asking each to invest at least $3,000 in the company.

Although all 31 members were investors and no outsiders held voting shares, the group of nine were the effective owners, and they elected four of seven directors. The employees elected the other three. In making the selection of 31 members, the purchasing group completely ignored the union (Amalgamated Meat Cutters and Butcher Workmen of North America) and the union contract.

The union and the company became embroiled in a bitter dispute which was brought before the Ontario Labour Relations Board (ORLB) in a controversial decertification hearing. The ORLB sided with the union, arguing that it retained bargaining rights because the Beef Terminal was not (as the purchasers claimed) a new company but a scaled-down version of an existing company. Furthermore, even in the revised operation, the workers were not effective owners but were employees of the purchasing group. The ORLB stated:

> Apart from their investment (amounting to $3,000 each), all of these employees are approximately in the same position, vis-a-vis their employee status, as they were when they worked for the predecessor . . . . They are paid a salary and are subject to the control and direction of management.[12]

In the view of the union, the employees "bought their jobs back." The Beef Terminal agreed to pay the union $31,000 in damages on behalf of 11 employees who, according to the contract, should have been given priority in joining the new company. In exchange, the union disbanded its bargaining unit at the Beef Terminal.

The ORLB's ruling on the Beef Terminal is somewhat inconsistent. While its point is well taken that the workers were primarily "employees" receiving direction from management, it also acknowledges that the employees had such ownership rights as representation on the Board of Directors and dividends from profits. The ORLB, therefore, used the term "employee-owners" in reference to the workers.

Although the Beef Terminal has some unique features, it follows in a tradition of management takeovers of failing firms. The Beef Terminal's manager, Jim Wilson, defends this structure vigorously: "it is absolutely mandatory to have continuity of management."[13]

Like so many other worker buyouts, the Beef Terminal had a limited lifespan. After some initial success, it became caught in another downturn in the packinghouse industry and in 1987 went into receivership. The company's assets were purchased by two private owners who retained many of the Beef Terminal's employees to operate the slaughterhouse.[14]

Celibec and Vent Air

Celibec[15] and Vent Air[16] were two different worker buyouts, one a computer services and manufacturing company in Trois Rivières, Québec, and the other a Winnipeg company that installs heating and ventilation systems. Both buyouts were made possible for one reason: Québec and Manitoba have government programs that provided the financing. Unless these companies had incorporated as co-operatives, government financing would not have been possible.

The Celibec buyout occurred prior to an actual shutdown. Its predecessor, Selin, a company owned by four engineers, found itself in financial difficulty. Two of the owners turned to a government agency, La Société de développement des coopératives (SDC), which was responsible for financing co-operatives. The SDC proposed that the company be converted into a worker co-operative. It offered administrative support and a long-term loan at 10 per cent. Thirteen of Selin's employees joined the co-operative and invested $5,000 each.

The new company, Celibec, took over the contracts, activities, and clientele of Selin. Three years after the takeover, sales increased from $600,000 to more than $3 million. The business, which originally focused on computer services, has been broadened so that a greater portion of the revenues comes from research and development and the production of computer software and hardware.

Celibec is channeling much of its business development into subsidiary companies, specialized in producing software for particular market sectors (e.g., medical offices). The membership in the co-operative has remained static, though the number of workers has increased to 40. It is reported, however, that Celibec which has recently invested $800,000 in the business is planning to add 15 new members.[17]

Vent Air of Winnipeg also became a worker co-operative because that structure was the most practical way to finance a business. When Vent Air's predecessor, Air Flow, went into receivership, two of its managers, Don Roy and Ralph Kubic, wanted to purchase it. After unsuccessfully approaching banks and the venture-capital program of the Federal Business Development Bank, they were told about the newly-established Manitoba Employment Co-operatives Program. They chose to involve the employees of Air Flow in the ownership structure of Vent Air because that was a way to obtain government loan guarantees to finance a buyout.

Ten of Vent Air's employees actually formed the co-operative in July 1985. The Board consists of five of these members, but the management style remains traditional. Also, because of the seasonal nature of Vent Air's work, there can be as many as 50 employees at any given time.

Vent Air took over the profitable portion of the old business, concentrating on commercial ventilation systems. In spite of the old business' image problems, Vent Air was able to take over all the major contracts except one. Sales, currently at about $3 million, have helped overcome the financial problems that beset Air Flow.

Like the old business, Vent Air is unionized (Local 511 of the Sheetmetal Workers Union). The union did not participate actively with management in organizing the buyout but supports it and maintains good relations with the co-op.

Pioneer Chainsaw[18]

A manufacturer of chainsaw powerheads and cutting attachments in Peterborough, Ontario, Pioneer Chainsaw, made the R.I.P. column in February 1985. Before that, the company had a short flirtation with employee ownership. The saga began in 1977 when Outboard Marine Corporation (OMC), an American conglomerate which had owned Pioneer for 20 years, announced that it was shutting down the plant and that 450 workers would lose their jobs. Outboard Marine Corporation claimed that it was losing over $5 million on the Peterborough operation.

The community, the union local (the United Steelworkers of America), and the workers rallied to prevent the closing and quickly developed a plan for a buyout. A numbered company was incorporated to bid on the plant, and a feasibility study was undertaken, financed by a federal government agency, the union, and the workers. The feasibility was positive, but the $7.6 million of financing was a problem. Enter Joe Mason, a Montréal entrepreneur who had previously engineered the successful Tembec pulp-and-paper mill buyout in Temiskaming. Mason put together the following financial package: The workers put up $128,000 in exchange for 24 per cent of the voting shares; Mason and his group put up $272,000 for 51 per cent of the voting shares; and the Federal Business and Development Bank (FBDB) put up $1.75 million for 25 per cent of the voting shares. The remaining financing was a $4.5 million term loan from a private lender, guaranteed by the Ontario Development Corporation (ODC) and the FBDB, and another $1 million loan from ODC. In other words, government agencies accepted the financial risk, and a private entrepreneur had effective control.

After its first year of operation, Pioneer broke even with sales of $17 million. A Swedish conglomerate, AB Electrolux, was seeking an entry into the North American market and offered $16.35 for Pioneer's shares which were issued for 50 cents a year earlier. Pioneer accepted the offer. "Workers make a million selling firm they saved," is the way a *Toronto Star* headline described the outcome. In fact, Local 8753 of the Steelworkers appealed unsuccessfully against the takeover to the Foreign Investment Review Agency (FIRA). Electrolux made promises to invest in and to expand the operation.

The rest of the story is all too familiar. Electrolux assumed control, eliminated Pioneer's European markets, shifted the R & D component to Sweden, and exported some of Pioneer's technology to its European subsidiaries. In February 1985, Electrolux closed the plant completely, and the 250 remaining workers lost their jobs. A portion of the production was moved to another Electrolux plant in London, Ontario.

The Granville Book Company[19]

At the beginning of 1986, the owner of the Mall Book Bazaar in Vancouver decided to close the business. The manager, Jim Allan, was given the opportunity to buy out the Mall.

Allan came up with financial plan that had each of the six employees of Mall, including himself, putting up $10,000 as part of a co-operative arrangement. This arrangement failed to work because three members of the group had no access to that kind of money, and two others had to borrow from the bank. Allan decided to go ahead on his own. After being turned down by regular banks, he negotiated a $30,000 loan from the Federal Business Development Bank (FBDB), and a distributor permitted him to take $72,000 of stock on credit.

Allan decided that he wanted the others involved; he now retains 52 per cent of the stock and two other employees hold the remainder. All staff participate in a profit-sharing plan and in decision-making. The store, now called the Granville Book Company, is doing well at last report.

Lessons

Each of the cases is different, and other cases could be cited that would add to the variety. Nevertheless, some common dimensions appear. Plant closings are seldom last-minute accidents, rather they result from decisions taken deliberately by the owners and are often planned in advance. Canada's branch-plant economy makes it very vulnerable to closings planned in foreign boardrooms. Investments in modernizing equipment are not made, profits are repatriated rather than invested in the plant, foreign markets are cut off, and eventually the plant becomes non-competitive and disposable.

It would, however, be oversimplistic to view plant closings simply as a result of either foreign ownership or private ownership in general. Plant closings are also a result of competitive market conditions, the overall state of the economy, world commodity prices, and interest rates. Many plants that are shut down are not worth reviving because the demand for the product or service no longer exists or the equipment has become so obsolete that it would require a major investment to modernize it.

Strategies have been devised that would prevent some plant closings from occurring. These include an early-warning system developed by the Midwest Centre for Labour Research in Chicago whereby that organization assists union locals to detect when a corporation is planning the shutdown of a particular plant and to initiate a political process to prevent the closure.[20]

A strategy undertaken by some labour federations is to create a venture-capital fund for investment in small and medium-sized businesses. These investments also stabilize those enterprises and provide organized labour with some influence over them. The $200 million Québec Solidarity Fund is probably the best example of such a strategy.[21] Tax credits in the February 1988 federal budget have spurred the Canadian Federation of Labour to establish its own fund,[22]and it is anticipated that others will follow. None of these strategies speaks directly to the issue of worker buyouts. They are simply to keep existing industries in business and to forewarn a union and its members when a closing is being planned.

Even when there is advance warning, a worker buyout is not necessarily the most practical option. The reasons are worth summarizing because they provide help in understanding why so few worker buyouts ever occur. First, as noted, when a plant is closed, it is usually because the prospects for success are not good: The plant is not turning a profit, the market assessment is not promising, or the plant requires a major investment in modernization for which a proper return is not anticipated. Of the cases reviewed in this chapter, Lamford was an exception. Its plants were in excellent shape and its reputation was good. The previous owners could not service the company's debt because of a sharp increase in interest charges and a decline in forest-product prices. The company was losing money but had potential if it could be rid of its debt burden.

Second, workers as a group are not prepared to become owners and have little interest in doing so. As a rule, the initiative for a buyout comes from senior management of the old company. Managers know the operation well and also know what parts of the overall operation can be salvaged. Many buyouts are, in fact, management buyouts. When workers become involved, it is usually because senior management lacks financing and requires workers' investment either to obtain bank loans or to become eligible for financing from a government program (as in Manitoba and Québec). At times, management may have benevolent motives as in the Granville Bookstore. The benevolent-owner syndrome is noteworthy -- and atypical. In spite of some opportunities that may have been missed, the general reluctance of workers to participate in buyouts is based upon a reasonable assessment of the facts. When a firm is being closed, the likelihood of a successful buyout is not good.

Third, in unionized firms, the leadership of the union is important in organizing a buyout. The union's initiative was important at Canadian Porcelain, Pioneer Chainsaw, and Lamford, and the union local had a passive role in the Vent Air buyout. Essentially, workers look to their union for leadership. As noted, Canadian unions have been very selective in their support of worker buyouts; the decision has been pragmatic and based on the probability of the buyout's success. The Victoria Plywood buyout was opposed because it was seen as unlikely to succeed and as detrimental to union wages in the forestry industry. Unions not only provide leadership to the workers but also are helpful in arranging financing for feasibility analyses. The Ontario Federation of Labour has lobbied the provincial government to legislate a compulsory feasibility analysis when a plant closing is announced.[23] However, the primary intention of this OFL initiative is not to encourage worker buyouts. The OFL is interested in keeping plants open and in preserving the union membership, whether the owners are private entrepreneurs or workers. Recently, the OFL has begun to view worker ownership as one possible way of accomplishing its goal,[24] but to date, it has not put much political muscle behind achieving it.

Fourth, financing is a major problem in any worker buyout,

even though the assets may be available at a discounted price once the company has passed into receivership. If a buyout is proposed prior to closing, then management is most likely to be the purchaser because it has the personal assets and the skill to leverage company assets as well as the knowledge to arrange financing. Once a company has passed into receivership, the workers are at an enormous disadvantage in arranging a purchase. Unlike a corporate competitor that might be interested in purchasing part of the assets, workers lack financing or ready access to lines of credit. Organizing small investments from a large group of anxious workers is a formidable undertaking. Corporations or private entrepreneurs, by contrast, can move much more quickly both in making a feasibility assessment and in arranging financing. In most attempts at worker buyouts, the financial arrangements are complex and burdened with debt. Often lending agencies will not look at the deal unless an established entrepreneur is involved (e.g., Pioneer). Even when the package can be assembled, the receiver is wary and is much more eager to accept a bid from an established corporation (e.g., Lapp in the Canadian Porcelain case, even though it contributed to the shutdown).

Fifth, when a worker buyout can be organized, maintaining the company as worker-owned can be problematic. As the example of the Beef Terminal illustrates, worker-owned firms are at risk in a competitive market. Pioneer Chainsaw illustrates that worker-owned companies also are subject to the problems of success. Workers, when they have the opportunity, may want to cash in their investment for personal profit. Also, successful worker-owned companies may have difficulty raising financing for expansion and may have to turn to outside investors who insist upon a degree of control. Both the failure and success scenarios are quite familiar.

When all of these factors are taken into consideration, it is not surprising that there are so few worker buyouts in Canada. Other countries have a different experience. In Italy, for example, buyouts are commonplace and have been organized primarily by the country's largest federation of worker co-operatives, the Lega, with the co-operation of both organized

labour and the state.[25]   In his analysis of Italian worker
co-operatives, Robert Oakeshott attributes the large number of
successful buyouts organized by the Lega to:

> . . . cheap credits under the privileges enjoyed by all Italian
> co-ops; and the congruence of the Lega's social and political
> objectives with those of Italy's main communist-controlled
> trade-union federation. Evidently, its rescue operations have
> normally been immune to the trade union hostility which, it is
> claimed, has thwarted the Confederation's (another worker
> co-op federation) efforts.[26]

In Canada, there is no similar commitment from either the
state or from organized labour, and there is, at present, no
association of worker co-operatives with the capacity to organize
buyouts in the same manner as Italy's Lega or France's SCOP
federation. As such worker buyouts operate in isolation from any
stabilizing influence or any system that is likely to assist their
maintenance as worker-owned. Governments have supported
worker buyouts as a last resort, preferring instead to assist
privately-owned buyouts with multi-million dollar grants and
interest-free loans. Outside of Québec and Manitoba, worker
buyouts can count on little financial support. This lack of support
by Canadian governments may be contrasted to American state
governments, particularly in New York, Michigan, and
Massachusetts, that have financed centres for employee
ownership and are attempting to preserve local industries under
employee ownership. New York State's recently-published
Cuomo Commission Report (named after Governor Mario Cuomo)
"recommends that employee ownership be made a central part of
state and national economic strategies."[27]

Similarly, in spite of particpating in an increasing number of
worker buyouts, organized labour in Canada has been very
cautious about encouraging worker ownership. Recently, there
appears to be some change in selected unions: Québec's
Confederation des syndicats nationaux (CSN), has a small
advisory group to assist its members in organizing worker
buyouts which are deemed feasible;[28] American locals in the
United Steelworkers of America have organized many buyouts in
the steel industry[29] and their president, Lynn Williams,[30] has
been very supportive of buyouts as one tool for combatting

potential shutdowns; and the International Woodworkers Association has been involved in several forestry-industry buyouts in British Columbia.[31]

Even though there has been some change, it would be misleading to say that either the Canadian or American labour movement is making worker buyouts a priority. Rather, labour is developing experience with buyouts, and, when challenged, appears willing to seriously consider the buyout alternative. Mechanisms are being put into place such as the AFL-CIO's buyouts' fund,[32] ongoing contact with business consultants who are familiar with worker ownership, and heightened vigilance to the early signs of an impending shutdown. Most noteworthy are some experiments in organizing worker purchases in companies not faced with closure. The best examples in Canada are the conversions to worker co-operatives of four privately-owned ambulance companies in the Montréal-Québec City corridor, organized by the CSN's advisory group.[33]

From Buyouts to Conversions

In contrast to buyouts which are last-minute rescue attempts, conversions involve workers becoming the owners of healthy companies. There are examples of owners who sell their business to their workers out of idealism. The classic example in Canada was the 1945 sale of Garden City Press in Montréal by its owner, James-John Harpell.[34] The new company, Harpell Press Co-operative, continues to prosper in the printing business with 200 employees and $12 million of sales (in 1986). Harpell was a visionary who like Robert Owen of New Lanark wanted to change the way work was organized. Others have walked down that path,[35] but evidence suggests that idealism will not inspire many owners to convert their enterprise to co-operative ownership. Conversions result from favourable government policies that provide incentives to both owners and interested workers. Because of the limited financial resources among workers a mechanism is needed to permit the gradual acquisition of shares by employees. The ESOP trust fund through which owners sell stock to their employees is one such mechanism. The ESOP has been used in the United States (see Chapter 1), and a variation of the American arrangement is being used in Britain where the union-controlled bank, Unity Trust, makes financing available for acquisitions.[36]

The ESOP is but one mechanism for financing a gradual transfer of ownership to the employees. The American ESOP has been criticized because most often (including cases where the trust fund holds a majority of the stock) the original owners retain corporate control. It is possible to have ESOP legislation without this shortcoming. It is also possible to establish mechanisms that encourage a gradual acquisition by employees through direct ownership rather than retaining the shares in a trust fund. This has occurred in France where about one-third of worker co-operatives formed in recent years have been conversions.[37] The reason for this is the flexibility of France's legislation that permits worker co-operatives to be incorporated under company law.

During a gradual acquisition of company shares the workers become investors with rights like those of non-worker investors. In a company that is being purchased gradually in order to create a co-operative structure the employee shareholding may be viewed as a "transitional arrangement." As employees gain assets in their workplaces, they also acquire a tool to make larger purchases and to gain eventual control. This argument was made by former United States Senator Russell Long in support of the American ESOP program, and it is equally applicable to gradual conversions to co-operative ownership. Long states:

> Capital ownership . . . is an opportunity historically reserved for a relatively few. That is due to the simple fact that the ownership of new wealth is largely a function of the ownership of existing wealth. The current structure of our most widely-used financing techniques ensures that the rich will, in fact, continue to get richer . . . .
>
> Most Americans lack assets to pledge as security for a loan to acquire income-producing capital; consequently those who do not now own are unlikely to own in the future.[38]

A positive feature of the American ESOP legislation is that employee shareholdings are sufficiently large to be levered for more substantial purchases. In Canada, by contrast, government programs encourage only small purchases and usually by individual employees. The Ontario plan, for example, allows employees to receive a grant equal to 15 per cent of the purchase price. The maximum grant is only $300.[39]

One method that could be used to increase employee shareholdings is to link bonus shares for employees with dividends for non-employee shareholders. Paul Derrick, a long-time British co-operator, makes this inventive proposal in a monograph which urges the British Labour Party to use common ownership as an alternative to government nationalization.[40] Derrick's proposal builds upon legislation that the Labour Party as the government introduced in 1978. This legislation permits companies to issue to employees bonus shares that would be tax-free and would result in a reduction of corporation tax. The subsequent proposal to link bonus shares and dividends recognizes the entitlement of employees to a share of surplus earnings and would also increase employee shareholdings immensely. Bonus shares, Derrick suggests, could also be issued to "funds" similar to those created in Sweden which benefit the broader community.[41]

Taxation Policy

Just as taxation policy has been an important stimulus to the concentration of corporate wealth, evidence suggests that it would be an important consideration in a conversions strategy. The American ESOP experience indicates that tax incentives can greatly encourage conversions of conventional companies to employee ownership. Essentially ESOPs have resulted from a series of tax amendments (1974, 1986) which have made it financially lucrative for the owners of privately-held companies to sell a portion or all of their stock to trust funds. One of the key ESOP features provides for the tax-free rollover of the proceeds from the sale of a business to either an ESOP or to a worker co-operative, provided the proceeds are reinvested within a year.[42] This arrangement is comparable to the tax laws governing mergers between companies. In those cases there is no tax on the shareholders unless they sell their stock resulting from the merger. ESOP tax provisions have encouraged owners coming to retirement and lacking an heir to sell to their employees without financial penalties. In fact, about one-half of ESOPs in the United States involve retiring owners.[43]

In France there is a high rate of conversions because a worker co-operative as a type of company has a preferred rate of capital gains tax and avoids the capital-tax transfer problems. Bonus shares issued to employees and allocations from surplus earnings to collective reserves also are tax-deductible for worker co-operatives in France.[44] By contrast, Canadian worker co-operatives (like co-operatives in general) have par value shares that do not appreciate in value like the shares in a privately-owned corporation. Shareholders in privately-owned corporations can realize up to $50,000 of capital gains without taxation. There is no similar tax benefit for members of worker co-operatives.[45]

In Québec there are indications that worker co-operatives are converting themselves into partnerships to gain tax advantages. In a study of Québec taxation, Jean-Claude Guerard, a professor at the University of Montréal, outlines a number of types of discriminatory tax.[46] These include taxation on surplus earnings retained in a collective reserve (even though members have no entitlement to the reserve) and taxation on dividends from surplus earnings because these are considered salaried earnings rather than investment income which receives a tax credit.

There are many ways of creating a favourable tax climate for worker co-operatives. Spanish tax law, for example, permits worker co-operatives to be tax-exempt for 10 years and subsequently to pay at a lower rate than privately-owned corporations.[47] (Under Spanish law, the credit co-operative, Caja Laboral Popular, can also give depositors a higher rate of interest.)

The lesson from all of these examples is that favourable tax policies encourage both the development of existing worker co-operatives and the conversion to co-operatives from other forms of ownership. A simple procedure to provide tax incentives for conversions, advocated by Derrick, would be to reduce the rate of corporation tax on worker-owned companies relative to other business corporations.[48] The problem is not technical but rather political, that is, putting together a coalition of support for tax policies that favour conversions. Such a proposal is not inconsistent with the tradition in Canada and other modern countries for using the tax system to encourage trends in economic development. There are a number of arguments in support of a conversions policy, though these are premised on the view that worker ownership is a positive objective. Given that all good people are not like-minded, we shall take the liberty of making the case.

A Final Thought

In the mid-nineteenth century Karl Marx argued that a fundamental aspect of capitalism was the conflictual relationship between two basic classes: the bourgeoisie who own the means of production and the workers who are employed by the bourgeoisie. The class warfare that Marx foresaw has not materialized -- if war is taken literally. On the other hand the relationship between workers and owners is not overly harmonious and is often very impersonal. With the exception of small businesses where the owner participates actively in the enterprise, workers and owners deal with each other through intermediaries, that is, managers appointed by the owners and labour representatives of the workers, each of whom tries to uphold the interests of their respective group. This arrangement often results in a lack of commitment from workers to the plant that employs them. It is also apparent that owners, particularly the shareholders of mature corporations, generally lack a commitment to their employees or to the employees' community. Decisions about maintaining and developing existing plants are made on the basis of corporate interest (i.e., investment decisions) not from the viewpoint of a community or its employees. As corporate holdings become more concentrated and divorced from particular enterprises, the differing interests of the shareholders and their employees are made more extreme.

Corporations have attempted to solve these difficulties through various techniques such as profit-sharing, bonus plans, employee perks, and token involvement of employees in decision-making. Japanese corporations, in particular, appear to be successful in building employee loyalty. It would be cavalier to dismiss as cosmetic all the techniques for improving employee commitment. Regardless of the type of ownership, worker alienation is a problem. Yet evidence suggests that it is much less of a problem where workers are the effective owners of enterprises in which they are employed. The reasons for this should not be a mystery. As owners, workers elect their board directors and may, if elected themselves, be members of the board; and as owners, workers derive the full value for their work. Salaries paid to worker and dividends paid to owners (either shareholders in a corporation or members in a co-operative) benefit the same people -- the workers. Unlike a privately-owned corporation, worker-owned companies do not have an inherent conflict between shareholders' and workers' interests.

Yet a political strategy is always embedded in a political reality. The political reality in advanced capitalist economies such as Canada's involves a very weak tradition for employee ownership and a very high concentration of capital and corporate control. In other words, even if employees were interested, they have very few assets to lever as part of a conversions strategy. A commitment from government is needed. Through taxation and other policies the government could enable groups of workers to become substantial shareholders in the company that employs them. As shareholders the workers would have the opportunity to use their equity to gain effective control where the circumstances are appropriate.

Governments are most likely to make that commitment where the closure of a plant would threaten a community or a large number of workers. A broad commitment for converting healthy companies to worker ownership has not been made. The Swedish wage-earner funds are the closest that any Western government has come to doing this.[49] These funds are an indirect form of worker ownership projected to eventually own five per cent of publicly-traded shares.

The Swedish funds are an experiment, and the results are being observed throughout the world by governments struggling with the increasingly complex dynamics of modern economies. It is not a coincidence that this experiment is occurring in Sweden where a social-democratic government has been at the forefront of innovation in developing the welfare state and is now dealing with the issues of economic democracy. The Swedish funds are but one example of the growing recognition that a prerequisite for economic democracy is economic ownership by workers, unions, and their local communities. A scaled-down version of this approach is the venture-capital funds being developed by Canadian labour organizations. In part, a defensive strategy to protect jobs, the venture-capital funds are also tools which could eventually be used to undertake bolder initiatives. Rather than being incompatible with the worker co-operative these various initiatives can be seen as different approaches to economic democracy.

The worker co-operative is a micro-experiment which provides a model for a particular workplace. It does not address the issue of transformation. That requires a political coalition which can create policies for bringing business assets under workers' control. Without that type of coalition, the worker co-operative remains but an isolated example of what is possible. The value of "possibilities" should not, however, be underestimated. Workers' accomplishments in fashioning a democratic workplace are vital if policymakers are to support initiatives that facilitate the creation of worker co-operatives.

Notes

[1]William Annett, "Brother, Can You Spare a Sawmill?" *Small Business*, December 1987, 34-40.

[2]John Faustmann, "When Workers Turn Bosses, *Report on Business*, March 1988, 41-48.

[3]Dana Weber, "Victoria Plywood Plant Restructured as a Worker Co-op," *Worker Co-op*, 5, No. 1 (1985), 9-10.

[4]Shane Simpson and Dana Weber, "A Union Viewpoint on Forestry Buyouts in B.C.," *Worker Co-op*, 5, No. 4 (1986), 12-14.

[5]See also Melanie Conn and Dana Weber, "Worker Buyouts in British Columbia," *Worker Co-op*, 8, No. 4 (1989), forthcoming.

[6]Melanie Conn and Dana Weber, "Co-op Wins National Award," *Worker Co-op*, 7, No. 3 (1988), 24.

[7]For analyses of Canadian Porcelain see Bob Schutte, "Canadian Porcelain Worker Buyout Thwarted," *Worker Co-op*, 5, No. 1 (1985), 14-16; and Murray Gardner, "The Canadian Porcelain Co-operative Story," *Co-op College Working Paper Series*, 4, No. 1 (1986), 57 pp.

[8]Bruce Little and Angela Barnes, "U.S. Firm Gets Takeover Nod," *Globe and Mail*, June 22, 1985, p. B4.

[9]"Lapp Insulators Closes Canadian Porcelain Plant," *Worker Co-op*, 7, No. 3 (1988), 27.

[10]Lynda Powless, "Lapp Willing to Sell Plant, $11.4-Million Price Mentioned," *Hamilton Spectator*, December 10, 1987, D2.

[11]Jack Quarter, "There's more than Beef at the Beef Terminal," *Worker Co-op*, 2, No.2 (1982), 5-6.

[12]Ontario Labour Relations Board Ruling on Amalgamated Meat Cutters and Butcher Workmen of North America A.F.L.-C.I.O.-C.L.C. and its Local P287 and the Beef Terminal (1979) Ltd., File No. 1818-79-R.

[13]Quarter, "There's more than Beef," p. 6.

[14]Judith Brown, Worker Buyouts in Ontario Have Mixed Results," *Worker Co-op*, 8, No. 4 (1989), forthcoming.

[15]Michael Lambert, "Celibec: a High-Tech Worker Co-operative," *Worker Co-op*, 6, No. 2 (1986), 38-30.

[16]Jeremy Hull, "Vent Air: the Phoenix Is Rising," *Worker Co-op*, 7, No. 3 (1988), 36-37.

[17]Claude Carbonneau, Québec Buyout Has Become a Successful Business," *Worker Co-op*, 8, No. 4 (1989), forthcoming.

[18]Bob Schutte, "The Pioneer Chainsaw Massacre: The Bitter Lessons of a Plant Shutdown," *Worker Co-op*, 5, No. 3 (1985), 14-15.

[19]Alan Twig, "Employee Ownership Breeds Bookstore Success," *Quill & Quire*, October 1987, Trade News Section.

[20]Greg LeRoy, *Early Warning Manual Against Plant Closings*, Working Papers, No. 2 (Chicago: Midwest Centre for Labour Research, 1986), 69 pp.

[21]"Québec Solidarity Fund", *Worker Co-op*, 7, No. 4 (1988), 18.

[22]"Labour Venture Fund," *Worker Co-op*, 8, No. 4 (1989), forthcoming.

[23]"Ontario Federation of Labour Submission to Ontario Legislative Committee on Plant Closures and Employee Adjustment," March, 1987.

[24]Gordon Wilson, "Speech Delivered at the NDP Municipal Conference," Toronto, April 30, 1988.

[25]Robert Paton, *Analysis of the Experience of and Problems Encountered by Worker Takeovers of Companies in Difficulty or Bankrupt* (Luxembourg: Commission of European Communities, 1987), 233 pp.

[26]Robert Oakeshott, *The Case for Workers' Co-ops* (London: Routledge & Kegan Paul, 1978), Chapter 9.

[27]Cited in "New Books Feature Employee Ownership," *The Employee Ownership Report*, VIII, No. 4 (1988), 4.

[28]Leopold Beaulieu, "Major Québec Labour Federation Starts Organizing Worker Co-operatives," *Worker Co-op*, 7, No. 3 (1987), 20-21.

[29]Warner Woodworth, "Re-Steeling the U.S.," *Worker Co-op*, 9, No. 4 (1989), forthcoming.

[30]Jack Quarter, "An Interview with Lynn Williams," *Worker Co-op*, 9, No. 4 (1989), forthcoming.

[31]Melanie Conn and Dana Weber, "Many Types of Worker Buyouts in British Columbia," *Worker Co-op*, 9, No. 4 (1989), forthcoming.

[32]Chris Meek, "Worker Buyouts on the Increase in the U.S." *Worker Co-op*, 9, No. 4 (1989), forthcoming.

[33]Claude Carbonneau, "Québec Labour Federation Develops Worker Co-ops," *Worker Co-op*, 8, No. 3 (1989), p. 25.

[34]Paul Vincent, "James-John Harpell: Pioneer of Worker Co-ops in Canada," *Worker Co-op*, 6, No. 4 (1987), 11-12.

[35]Ernest Bader of the Scott-Bader Company is an excellent example in Britain.

[36]Norma Henderson, "ESOPs Become Popular as a Buyout Tool in Britain, *Worker Co-op*, 8, No. 4 (1989), forthcoming.

[37]Chris Axworthy, *Worker Co-operatives in Mondragon, the U.K. and France: Some Reflections* (Saskatoon, Sask.: Centre for the Study of Co-operatives, 1985).

[38]Russell Long, "Proceedings and Debates of the 98th Congress, First Session," *Congressional Record*, Washington, Thursday, November 17, 1983, p. 10.

[39]"Employee Share Ownership Plan," Toronto: Ontario Ministry of Revenue, 1988.

[40]Paul Derrick, *The Labour Party and Common Ownership* (London, England: The Committee for Socialist Renewal, 1985), 22 pp.

[41]*Employee Investment Funds* (Stockholm: Ministry of Finance, 1984).

[42]Russell Long, "Employee Ownership and Better Labour-Management Relations," *Congressional Record*, Washington, Friday, June 29, 1984, p. 3.

[43]Corey Rosen, "U.S. Tax Law Encourages Employee Ownership," *Worker Co-op*, 6, No. 3 (1987), 6-8.

[44]Derrick, *The Labour Party and Common Ownership*.

[45]Brian Iler, "Worker Co-op Taxation," *Worker Co-op*, 7, No. 3 (1988), 4.

[46]Jean-Claude Guerard, "Taxation: Do Worker Co-ops Pay too Much?" *Worker Co-op*, 7, No. 2 (1987), 14-16.

[47]Axworthy, *Worker Co-operatives in Mondragon, the U.K. and France*.

[48]Derrick, *The Labour Party and Common Ownership*.

[49]*Employee Investment Funds*.

Chapter 4

Co-operative Farming:
A Model For Worker Ownership
in Agriculture

George Melnyk

"Hey John, How's the Crop?" is the title of a large print by the Edmonton artist, Harry Savage. On a barren, brown field stands an aging farmer in black rubber boots, a red cap, and an ill-fitting purple jacket. Above him is a sparkling blue sky and a magnificent rainbow. The message is clear -- for the farmer hope springs eternal even in the worst conditions.

The current crisis in North American agriculture has removed that optimistic rainbow from above the heads of many farmers.[1] Indebtedness, drought, low commodity prices, soil degradation, and just plain despair about the future are driving increasing numbers of farmers off their land. The current farm crisis simply accelerates a trend that has been firmly established since the Second World War. The trend means fewer farmers and fewer farms. Large operations are touted as the form of economic viability in agriculture. The marketplace sees agri-business as the only model with a future.

The endless cycles of government subsidies to agriculture have not stopped the reduction in the number of farms and farmers. Certain operations survive on life-support systems until the plug is pulled, and in the end it always is.

Forty years ago, when mechanized farming began to revolutionize prairie agriculture in a significant way, there was an attempt to use co-operative principles and social ownership to create a model of agricultural production that was different from the all-pervasive, private-sector family farm. This experiment occurred in Saskatchewan and came to be known as the "co-op farm" movement. It was the first widespread and sustained application of worker co-op principles in Canadian agriculture. The lessons from this experiment provide a valuable contribution to the debate on worker ownership.

On a co-op farm the members held equal shares in the enterprise. Each member had one vote, was paid monthly wages based on the hours worked, and at the end of the year received any dividends declared proportionate to the hours worked. The co-op farm provided medical and disability insurance, paid holidays, and a pension plan. The Rochdale rules were strictly adhered to, with membership being voluntary and capital receiving a limited return. Other than the fact that the work was farm work and co-operative farmers generally lived in a small community, there was no appreciable difference between a worker co-op and a co-op farm. Their governance and co-op structures were similar.

Co-operative farming was unique to Saskatchewan and has survived since the Second World War, albeit in a modified form. This experiment provides a model for worker ownership in agriculture, which has both positive features and pitfalls. No serious attempt to establish worker co-ops in agricultural production is possible without reflection on the co-op farm experience in Saskatchewan. When some Alberta farmers attended an agricultural symposium in 1987, they were told by a Saskatchewan academic and farm expert that they ought to band together to form "integrated agricultural enterprises" that were community-owned.[2] The speaker appealed to the prairie tradition of wheat pools and marketing boards as group enterprises that could be realized in production rather than just marketing. It is that tradition which provided the crucial context for this radical experiment in co-operative farming.

The Tradition

Ian MacPherson, the eminent historian of Canadian co-operation, described the co-operative model as having "seized the imagination of the Prairie farmer."[3] Out of this enthusiasm developed powerful instruments of co-operation such as the wheat pools, the credit union movement, and co-operatively-owned retail stores. Saskatchewan's agrarian economy was the basis of this agrarian co-operative movement because it was an economy built on a pyramidal structure with a multitude of small family-farmers at its base, who felt exploited and abused by the marketplace. Beginning with farmer-owned grain elevators and ending with the wheat pools spawned in the mid-1920s, the prairie farm producers were, by the Second World War, accustomed to using co-operative structures to advance their interests. This was particularly true of Saskatchewan, which had a particularly potent co-operative movement, exemplified by Canada's first co-operative refinery built in Regina in the mid-thirties.[4]

The co-operative tradition was linked to political radicalism through its association with the Co-operative Commonwealth Federation (CCF), which held its founding convention in Regina in 1933, where it issued its famous "Regina Manifesto" calling for the creation of a co-operative commonwealth. The CCF was democratic socialist in orientation, which meant it was committed to parliamentary democracy, state intervention, and support for the economic underdog. In 1944 it was the people of Saskatchewan who elected the CCF as the provincial government, thereby creating North America's first democratic socialist administration. Western Canadian historian, Gerald Friesen, has termed this election the choosing of "a new path;"[5] while the American social scientist, Seymour Lipset, termed it "the culmination of a half-century of political and economic efforts by western grain growers to establish a stable economy."[6] The election was viewed by its winners and its losers as a new beginning, as the triumph of populist pressure for a new deal.

The CCF government's commitment to co-operative development was genuine and inspired by its radical roots. It immediately established Canada's first ministry of Co-operation and Co-operative Development to foster and expand co-operative enterprise in the economy. One of its more novel initiatives was the promotion of co-operative farming. A 1947 photograph shows the Premier, Tommy Douglas, and several cabinet ministers attending the first anniversary celebrations of one of the newly-formed co-op farms. The celebrations attracted 3,000 well-wishers.[7] From this one would imagine there was a massive groundswell, a kind of agrarian revolution. However, this was not the case. Unlike the frantic election of the Social Credit Party in Alberta during the height of the Depression, the election of the CCF represented a more studied sense of reform. The economy of 1944 was not the desperate one of 1935, nor was capitalism in a state of crisis as it had been before the war. The mood was not one of collectivist euphoria but of expanding expectations.

The co-op farm movement was born in a tradition that valued what may be called "liberal-democratic" co-operation.[8] This is a strictly Rochdale form of co-operation that is unifunctional, market-oriented, and non-interfering with the private-property holdings of its members. Consumer co-operation and farm-producer marketing co-ops were the norm. Co-op farms represented a significant step beyond that reality. It was the election of a radical government which saw its mandate as one of socio-economic innovation and pushed co-operation beyond its liberal-democratic tradition. The results were not as grand as first envisaged.

First Steps

Armed with a pro-co-operative ideology and an electoral mandate, the CCF government interpreted the popular will as a call to set in motion the creation of the co-operative commonwealth. Within a few months of being elected, the government held a conference in Regina on the topic of co-operative farming, a concept which was being actively promoted in the summer of 1944 by the CCF party press.[9] The great excitement of the time, generated by the electoral breakthrough and the legitimacy offered by state support, attracted people to the concept, especially veterans who were looking for opportunities to resettle.

Lorne Dietrick, a pioneer of the co-op farm movement and one of its staunchest supporters and ideologues, describes his initial involvement in this way:

> In the winter of 1945 the Government made available the first tract of provincially-owned land for veterans' co-op farms. This was the old Matador ranch in southwestern Saskatchewan. The future members of the Matador co-operative farm came together at a conference held in Regina, April 6-9, 1946. . . . Fifty veterans attended. We were told that each veteran was entitled to 480 acres in southern Saskatchewan and 320 acres in the north. . . . Lockey MacIntosh, the first minister of the newly-formed Department of Co-operation, J.H. Sturdy, Minister of the Department of Reconstruction and Rehabilitation, Tommy Douglas, Premier, as well as university and experimental farm personnel spoke at the conference.[10]

So it was not just one conference in 1945, but other government-sponsored conferences that kept the process going. Lorne Dietrick's experience would be typical of the veterans who came to co-op farming.

Shortly after their development, co-op farms came under the general rubric of "production co-ops," which remained their classification with the Department of Co-operation and Co-operative Development. Eventually, this name was used to represent the movement as a whole, when the Saskatchewan Federation of Production Co-operatives was formed in the late 1940s. Production co-ops signified a number of different arrangements including: machinery co-ops in which individual farmers used co-operatively-owned machinery to work the land and harvest, co-operatively-owned or administered pastures for the grazing of livestock, hog-production co-ops, fur co-operatives for trappers, farmers that reared animals for their skins, and finally, the full co-operative farm. Of all these arrangements, it was the full co-operative farm that captured the political and social imagination of the day. It was viewed as the vanguard of the co-operative commonwealth, the perfect model of co-operative work and living to which true co-operators ought to aspire. It was to set the standard for co-operative ownership in agriculture and represent the co-operative ideals of the new government. This was a heavy burden and one that co-op farms were unable to carry.

Because co-op farming was promoted by the government as a scheme for the resettlement of veterans, the federal government's program of aid to veterans called the Veterans Land Act came into play. The Act provided for crown land and monetary grants to veterans who wanted to start farming. However, the federal government insisted that only veterans planning to farm individually would be eligible for this aid. The goal was to promote private farming not co-operatives. The pooling of grants was not allowed. So the provincial government extended loans to those veterans who wanted to farm co-operatively until such time as the federal government reversed its decision. Within two years this had been achieved, but even though the pooling of grants was allowed, ownership of the land had to remain individual and private, at least until such time as the 10-year option to buy was exercised.

To overcome the problem of individual ownership on a co-op farm, the veterans had an agreement with the provincial government that it would provide equivalent land should a member want to take his or her land and farm privately. The co-op farm was established by leasing these individual land holdings to the co-op and when the 10-year period was over and each member had clear title, the land was brought into the co-op as the member's capital contribution.

When the veterans' co-ops were being established, the provincial government recommended that a "farm manager" be hired to supervise the work and oversee the operation. The position would be comparable to a hired manager in a worker co-op or a general manager hired by a consumer co-op. The most famous of the co-op farms, Matador, refused to go along with this suggestion and opted to run its affairs totally by its own membership. This confidence in their ability to manage their affairs was rooted in the relatively small membership (initially 20), the common "being-your-own-boss" tradition among farmers, and a concern over state-interference in farm decision-making that some felt the government-appointed manager represented.

The commitment of co-op farmers to full democratic leadership and management is one of the major legacies of the movement. It meant that they had only themselves to praise when they made the right decisions and only themselves to blame if their decisions were wrong.

Even with the financial, legal, and administrative structures established, the co-op farmer still had to face the challenge of making the enterprise profitable. In the case of the veterans' co-ops, there were the additional problems associated with breaking virgin soil and constructing a farm community. It was a pioneering effort. In his memoirs, Lorne Dietrick describes his first days on the 10,000-acre Matador co-op farm:

> . . . we signed our veteran's papers for $75 per month for one year and free medical care. We then divided into two groups: one to break the land and the other to cut the H-hut at the Swift Current airport into 15 by 30 sections for transport to the farm.
>
> I was in the construction crew. We set up a kitchen and living quarters in the building while we cut the remainder into twelve 15 by 30 sections (two made a house). . . .We spent one month doing this. Loading and unloading these sections was very heavy work.[11]

Because Matador was located in the southwest of the province, the land did not have to be cleared of bush as did the co-op farms in the northeast. Life at Matador was easy compared to these agricultural outposts of the north.

There were five veterans' co-op farms established in the northeast in what was called the Carrot River district. The project was very large, covering 60,000 acres of provincially-owned land that was originally the Pasquia Forest Reserve. The Saskatchewan farm journalist, Jim Wright, termed the process of clearing the land "arduous work."[12] Photographs of the project showed bulldozers clearing the land and the construction of homes for the 140 people -- men, women, and children -- who pioneered these co-ops. The photographs provide a striking insight into the trials the farm co-operators faced and the spirit that must have animated them to carry on. The map in Figure 4-1 shows the location of the dozen full co-op farms established as of November 1, 1948.

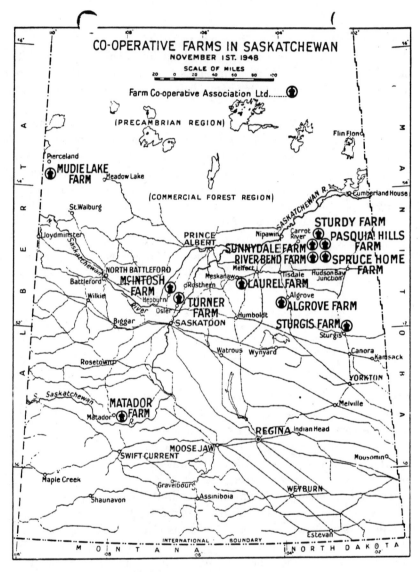

Figure 4-1: Location of co-op farms, November 1, 1948.
Reprinted from *Co-operative Farming in Saskatchewan* (Regina, Sask. Govt. Publication, 1949) p. 15.

The Dream Matures

The time from 1944 to 1952 was both the inauguration period and the heyday of the co-op farm movement in terms of public profile, the number of new farms being incorporated annually, and the government's commitment to the concept. This period coincided with the first two terms in office for the CCF government, which remained in power for 20 years. From 1945 to 1950, 17 co-op farms were incorporated with a total membership of 181 and an average membership of 11.[13] Considering that the farm population of Saskatchewan stood at 399,473 in 1951, the number of farm co-operators is statistically insignificant.[14] The total assets of these 17 co-ops stood at $500,000 and they owned, leased, or rented 59,000 acres.[15]

After 1952 the co-op farm movement began to decline. From a high of 32 co-op farms in 1952, only 21 remained by 1964. While co-op farms declined, the total number of production co-ops rose dramatically from 52 in 1949 to 313 in 1964.[16] It is clear that the limited forms of co-operation such as machinery and pasture-sharing were popular throughout the CCF's reign, while the co-operative communities represented by co-op farms had peaked early.

The lifestyle of full co-op farms offers a clue to why these farms were relatively unpopular compared to the limited forms of production co-ops. Henry Cooperstock studied co-op farms in the 1950s, and he provided an excellent description of how life on the co-op farm was organized:

> Typically, the enterprise consists of a number of families living in individual homes that are grouped in a fairly compact dwelling area situated on an acre or half an acre of the farm-site. The men work co-operatively on the land, which may be in a continuous piece or in several scattered parcels. Except in the co-operatives organized by veterans . . . the land is generally owned or leased by the group as a whole rather than by individuals. The male members meet once a week, sometimes less often, to plan the over-all farm operation and to allocate work. Some of the men may be doing chores, others working in the fields, and still others erecting storage granaries.
>
> The men draw equal monthly wages, regardless of the type of

> work they do, and at the end of the fiscal year the surplus is
> divided among them in proportion to the number of days of
> labour contributed by each . . . .
>
> In most cases the houses are owned by the co-operative
> association, but the living arrangements are similar to those
> on the individual farm; there are no communal kitchens or
> laundries and even the vegetable gardens generally are
> individual concerns. With few exceptions the women have no
> farm chores assigned to them and are either not members of
> the association or only nominal members and have no formal
> influence in the decision-making process. The role of the wife
> is thus more like that of the town housewife than of the
> average farm wife . . . .[17]

The members not only worked together on a daily basis the way they would in a worker co-op in the city, but they also lived together as neighbours. Their children would go to the same school and in some cases the school was located right on the co-op farm (as it was at Matador). This intense community life required adjustment and could accentuate personality differences that might be ignored in a larger, less involving setting. In the farm culture of Saskatchewan with its stress on the individual family farm and the general conservatism of the 1950s, the kind of social existence promulgated by co-operative farming would have a limited appeal.

This view must be balanced with the appeal that an instant community would have to war veterans who were accustomed to the comradeship of the military service or the family farmers who pooled their land with their neighbours and relatives to form a co-op farm. The social aspects of co-op farming were simultaneously a powerful glue and a force for disengagement, depending on the member. The pressures of the culture in which they lived were such as to limit the appeal of co-op farms to the adventuresome and the idealistic.

The limited size of individual co-op farm communities was a very serious problem when divisive issues arose. In a liberal-democratic co-operative structure like the Saskatchewan Wheat Pool with tens of thousands of members, the loss of a thousand or so is not a problem, especially when that number is replenished by new members joining on a continuous basis. It is the same with a large urban credit union, whose membership is constantly changing. The institution does not suffer. But in an 11-member co-op farm and a movement with a total membership of 200, the strain caused by people leaving and new people coming in is much higher. For co-op communities the issue is not statistical but personal. At Matador co-op farm a crisis of departure developed in 1956 when the veterans gained ownership of their land from the government and several members decided to take their land and leave. In an article about Matador written several years after the event, the journalist Idaville Melville, quotes one of the co-op women as saying, "We can't get used to losing Ruby and Beth. . . . All of us feel as if a part of the life was torn from Matador. It wasn't the women's fault. If it hadn't been for the women on the farm, we might have lost more in this crisis."[18]

Considering the tightly-woven nature of co-op farm life and the bonds it generated among its members, it is to the credit of the community that it was able to survive for a long period. Co-op farms did provide a higher standard of living for its members once the operation was well-established and pioneering work was over. The degree of modernity found on co-op farms made life easier in a material sense and the bonding that occurred in the democratic process was particularly important for the men. When the Saskatchewan journalist, Dennis Gruending, visited Matador in 1972, he was able to report that the fundamental organizational structure of the co-op farm had remained in place for a quarter of a century:

> Farm and financial decisions are made in group meetings by a majority vote of the co-operative's full members. . . . The farm never has needed a director . . . each member is paid an hourly wage . . . an hour's work draws an hour's pay regardless of the task. Each member submits a record of his labor hours . . . .

> Annual dividends are paid on the basis of the member's working hours for the year and on his equity capital at five per cent. Declaration of dividends is a group decision . . . .

> A health and accident program exists. A member will not lose any pay after the first ten days of sickness or misfortune. They have had a pension plan since 1950.[19]

The motivation for joining a co-op farm was studied early on by the sociologist of co-operation, Henrik Infield, who visited

Saskatchewan in 1946 and prepared a study on the members of Matador. He found that economic considerations were the main factor. "After quitting service," he wrote, "they just wanted to get started in farming and could not obtain land at a reasonable price."[20] However, Infield also discovered that the lure of community life was also important for these veterans. Most of the members were young and single and wanted the comradeship of co-operative enterprise.

Of the 20 co-op farms in existence in 1950, nine were veterans' co-ops and the remainder were non-veteran.[21] As time went by the number of non-veteran co-ops increased and they eventually evolved into family co-op farms, whose membership was based on kinship.[22] In fact, the first co-op arm incorporated in Saskatchewan was non-veteran. This was the Sturgis Co-operative Farm, which Lorne Dietrick, a member of Matador and temporarily employed by the Department of Co-operation, visited in 1948 and described in the following manner:

> I left for Sturgis arriving at the Sturgis co-operative farm in the afternoon. . . . That evening Charlie Mitchell, farm manager, was there and we discussed co-operative farming from the experience we all had. They were pleased with what had been accomplished. . . . They were building three houses on . . . the site a quarter of a mile from town. . . . For the next year they plan to build three more houses to accommodate the rest of the members . . . .
>
> To date they have fourteen members, seven men and their wives. I was pleased to see the active part taken by the women members and I am sure co-operative farming will benefit a lot from women being members.[23]

Another non-veteran co-operative farm was the Laurel Farm Co-operative Association incorporated in 1946. Its members included a father, son, and father-in-law who were operating three individual farms. The sons were also made members with contributions of $1,000 while the established farmers brought in much more. The goal was to equalize loan capital at $20,000 per member over a number of years.[24]

The evolution of co-op farming into a family enterprise reflected the social dimensions of farm life and the relative ease with which family members could come together to form co-operative enterprises. It would seem that the family farm organized as a co-operative fit the social landscape of Saskatchewan more easily than co-op farms composed of non-kinship groupings.

The evolution of co-op farming was monitored by the provincial government (by special reports) in the early years and then by the Department of Co-operation on an annual basis. The government could not help but notice that these co-operative communities were attracting few adherents. For example, in 1962 grazing or pasture co-operatives had a membership of 1,460 farmers grazing 32,000 head of cattle on 580,000 acres, while co-op farmers were only several hundred and declining in numbers.[25] Like all democratically-elected governments, the CCF was aware of the very limited vote-getting appeal of co-op farming. Instead it would focus on the demands and requirements of mass organizations like the Wheat Pool, which had sprung into being in the mid-twenties when 50 per cent of wheat producers in the province joined in a single year.[26] Compared to the roar of thousands of farmers clamouring for a co-op marketing scheme for their grain, the co-op farm movement was a whimper.

The establishment of political priorities other than co-op farming was already evident as early as 1949. A confidential government report prepared in 1949 stated that ". . . the greatest barrier to the formation of co-op farms is lack of capital necessary to purchase land and machinery." The report went on to suggest that ". . . a fund of $1,000,000 should be established for next year's operation."[27] Needless to say, the fund was never established. The problem of how new, unlanded farmers could set up a co-op was not solved. In 1949 only veterans receiving land under the Veterans Land Act and established farmers pooling their land were able to set up co-op farms. When crown land dried up, the only group capable of establishing co-op farms were farmers who were primarily interested in family connections. This was a serious limitation on the expansion of co-op farming among non-kinship groups.

As for the novelty of co-op farming being a barrier to its popularity, we need only compare this comment from the 1949 co-op farm conference: "Neighbouring farmers had a great deal of misinformation on the setup, particularly with regard to the relationship between the farm and the government," with this recent statement about the worker co-op concept: "The great majority of American citizens know nothing about worker co-operatives."[28]   Ignorance and misinformation are powerful barriers to attracting adherents to a voluntary social experiment.

The obstacles to the co-op farm movement's continued expansion can be summarized as follows:

1. problems surrounding land tenure created by the Veterans Land Act;

2. the gradual dropping off of provincial government support;

3. the pressures inherent in co-operative community life;

4. the lack of capital for start-ups;

5. the negative attitudes toward co-op farming among the predominant private-sector farmers;

6. the failure of the movement to reach a sufficient size or critical mass to generate its own momentum; and

7. the difficulty of maintaining a reality that was beyond the norms of the liberal-democratic co-operative tradition.

These obstacles did not destroy the co-op farm movement. However, the impediments, when taken as a whole, created a braking force which first slowed the movement and then caused its gradual transformation into a co-operative version of the family farm.

Passing on the Flame

The problem of equity formation, including the passing on of an expensive asset to the next generation, was an issue that co-op farms faced. When the 10-year option to own Veterans Act land came up for the members of the Matador co-op farm, several decided to leave with the land to which they had just received title. The provincial government had promised to replace the land taken out by departing members with comparable land in the district, but it was unable to honour this promise in 1956, so the size of Matador was reduced. In 1956 the land was valued at $40 per acre by the co-op, and this value was not meant to be speculative. Vic Hay, who joined Matador in 1959, wrote in a brief to an arbitration hearing concerning the valuation of land for another departing member that "no increase in price took place in the period between when retiring members left (1956) and when we came in. It is evident that the old members made no effort to speculate on the land at our expense."[29] This good will did not preclude arguments over land values when a member left.

This problem came to a head at Matador when the members became concerned about how the farm could be passed on to the next generation so as not to burden the new members with a massive debt and yet provide a return to the retiring members commensurate with their years of contribution to the value of the farm. The answer came when the New Democratic government of Allan Blakeney established a Land Bank to facilitate land transfer to the next generation without impoverishing it. The Land Bank bought the land of a retiring farmer and then leased it to his designated descendant with an option to purchase after five years. It was the Land Bank Commission itself that determined the value of the land and so removed it from the realm of legal disagreement over valuation. When John Messer, Saskatchewan's Minister of Agriculture, announced the Land Bank's purchase of Matador Co-op Farm in 1974, he was quoted as saying:

> This is a most important step in solving the transfer problem inherent in co-operative farm enterprises. In the past those members who wished to retire had found it nearly impossible to agree on land values to determine the equity of each member. The involvement of the Land Bank eliminates this problem.[30]

At Matador, a new co-operative called the Matador Farm Pool, was incorporated. It was composed of sons of the retiring members plus several others. The retiring members, who received their equity over a period of time for tax purposes, were allowed to remain in their homes at Matador if they wished. In a 1983 interview, Lorne Dietrick explained the importance of the Land Bank solution to co-op farming:

> A proper land tenure program should be a long-term use-lease system of land holding, which means that land would be used as a resource rather than a a commodity. . . .Every time we have to pay for that land that payment has to come out of production. If you had a long-term program of land tenure you wouldn't have to refinance the land every time it changes hands . . . .
>
> The Land Bank program in Saskatchewan was the only method that we could use to transfer this farm to the next generation. . . .I think there should be no right of purchase in a Land Bank lease to a co-operative.[31]

The co-op farm at Beechy, which was Matador's neighbour, did not pass on its holdings to the next generation. It sold out to private interests, who in turn sold the land to Hutterites for a new colony. The consolidated land holdings of co-op farms were attractive to these communal farmers.

The solution to the land problem in co-op farms has implications for industrial worker co-ops. In an industrial worker co-op, the capital expenditures could be the responsibility of a larger entity such as a trade union, a community development corporation, the government or a non-profit society, which would lease the "means of production" to the worker co-op. This would limit the cost of a worker joining a co-op, just as the Land Bank freed the new generation of farmers from a massive burden of debt.

Comparisons

The co-op farm movement was a failure when compared to the Hutterites, who are the world's largest religious agricultural-communal movement. They occupy 240 colonies in the three prairie provinces, have over 20,000 inhabitants, and are considered in the forefront of agricultural production.[32] There are sectors of private agriculture that see them as a threat because of their continuous expansion. The Hutterites only came to Western Canada after World War I, yet their impact on the region's agriculture has been significant. For example, Hutterites established a high-tech hog-slaughtering operation in Neepawa, Manitoba, in 1986, which employed 150 workers. At the time, the Hutterite colonies were producing about a third of Manitoba's total hog production.[33]

It is not my intention to provide a detailed comparison of the two movements. Suffice it to say that in agriculture, Western Canada had both a very successful liberal-democratic movement in the Wheat Pools and a very successful communal movement in the Hutterites. However, the co-operative farms that stood in the middle between these two extremes did not flourish.

In attempting to understand why the movement did not succeed over a long period of time, it is valuable to reflect on the general life cycle of co-operatives. In my book, *The Search for Community*, I argued that co-operatives went through a three-phase cycle. The first phase is called "utopian" and it is characterized by its idealism and its experimental nature. The second phase is the "movement" phase in which a particular co-operative form is adopted in a variety of places and undergoes rapid expansion in numbers. The third phase is "systems" in which the movement becomes bureaucratized, hierarchical, and consolidated. According to this model, the co-op farms of Saskatchewan did not go beyond the utopian phase of co-operative development. This does not mean that they were a minor historical blip. Rather they did not multiply sufficiently to go into the movement phase.

Trapped in the utopian phase, the co-op farms can be viewed in the same manner as other co-operative community experiments that did not become widespread and therefore withered. In a sense, they represented what Robert Owen's New Lanark was to the Rochdale pioneers. Individual participants may have benefitted but co-operative development in the region was not influenced significantly by their existence, even over several decades. Nevertheless, they have become part of the co-operative mythology of the region, referred to more with a sense of fond hope than hard-nosed pragmatism.

Analysis of Underdevelopment

The co-op farm was the brainchild of the CCF. It did everything that it could to nurture its baby during its first four years. But this enthusiasm waned as more pressing political priorities came to the fore, and the child was asked to walk on its own before it was mature enough to do so. The result was stunted development. But it would be unfair to blame the CCF for the failure of co-op farms to go beyond the utopian stage. As I have argued in more detail elsewhere, the CCF was simply being true to the dictates of political reality in a parliamentary democracy.[34] Nor can the individual co-op farmers or the co-op farm concept as such be blamed for the failure to grow. The record shows that they made a major effort and persisted through a variety of difficulties; they eventually overcame numerous legal, organizational, and social obstacles. Likewise, the cultural milieu of the day was a problem but not an insurmountable barrier to expansion.

The significant and overriding factor in their stunted growth was the historic trend of rural depopulation and agri-business development. Between 1931 and 1961 there was a 23 per cent decline in farm population in Saskatchewan and an increase in the average size of family farms from 408 to 686 acres.[35] In 1941, 60 per cent of the workforce in Saskatchewan was engaged in agriculture; by 1961 it had dropped to 48 per cent; and by 1971 to 26 per cent.[36] The trend continued with a drop to 18 per cent in 1981.

This kind of mega-trend could not leave co-op farming unaffected. Using the example of the Matador co-op farm, we find that of the original 20 members who came together in 1946, there were 18 by 1952; and when the farm was passed on in 1974, membership was down to 11. This reduction in numbers parallels the drop in the number of Saskatchewan farmers from about 130,000 in 1945 to 60,000 in 1985.[37] In other words, co-op farms underwent a decline in numbers comparable to that of private farms. That initial boost that the government provided in the 1944 to 1952 period was a counterweight to the historic trend. But once the government left the movement on its own, the basic pattern affecting all prairie agriculture reasserted itself.

Of course, one can point to the Hutterites and claim that they are an example of a sect that has bucked the historical tide. Unlike the Hutterites, the co-op farmers were victims of the same trends that affected the private sector. In its 1984 study of the prairie economy, the Economic Council of Canada described agriculture as "a net drag" on Western Canada's economic growth in the 1972 to 1982 period.[38] The declining value of agriculture to the prairie economy meant that co-op farming was operating in a sector of the economy that was on the skids. The growth industries were oil, gas, potash, pulp, and uranium; co-op farming was not part of the major engines of growth. It is difficult for any co-operative reality, liberal-democratic or otherwise, to flourish and expand when it is part of a troubled industry. Of course, this decline was not visible in the 1940s and 1950s when co-op farming held out promise and agriculture was the workhorse of the prairie economy. But with hindsight, one can see clearly that co-op farming, like the family farm, was a victim of historic trends.

The continued survival of the co-op farm concept in Saskatchewan in the form of a family enterprise suggests that its relevance is not completely lost. For example, the Self-Reliance and Hard Struggle co-op farm of Sonningdale was incorporated in the early seventies as a product of the counterculture, but a decade later it had become a family co-op. It is clear that kinship provides a bond of survival, a meaningful impetus for continuation which the non-kinship co-op farm has not been able to provide. The family co-op farm fits the social landscape of Saskatchewan's rural community. This variant of the co-op farm has remained alive because it is a wedding of the co-op and the family-farm tradition.

Lessons for Worker Co-ops

The lessons that the co-op farm movement has to offer worker co-ops are both positive and negative. On the positive side there is the powerful democratic tradition found in the organizational structure of co-op farming. The economic provisions for equal pay, pension plans, health insurance, and paid vacations, which were so novel for the private farmer of the day, are important hallmarks of mutual responsibility and worker ownership. Co-op farms showed that co-operative principles were well-adapted to production in agriculture. It was not the co-op principles that caused the movement to flounder but factors in the general climate over which the co-op had no control.

On the negative side, the history of co-op farming points out that state-co-operative relations are, in Ian MacPherson's words, "an uneasy alliance."[39] To paraphrase a well-known religious saying, "What the state has given, the state taketh away." Although government support can be crucial to launching and sustaining a social experiment, that support can create a dependency syndrome, both psychological and material, which inhibits a movement from becoming self-supporting and self-expanding. A contemporary example of this problem is the co-operative housing movement in Canada, which grew spectacularly in the 1970s and early 1980s under the social-housing program of Canada Mortgage and Housing. In only 15 years the movement grew to have a 100,000 members. But when the Liberal administration in Ottawa, under which the program was established, was changed to a Conservative one in 1984, this expansion was cut back drastically. Mark Goldblatt, Executive Director of the Co-operative Housing Foundation, described the lack of a self-financing infrastructure for co-op housing as "a hair-raising experience which is not worth repeating in the worker co-op sector."[40]

Although some co-op farmers may have come to feel that they were betrayed by the CCF government, it is unfair for any volunteer-based co-operative movement to blame the state for its unpopularity unless the state deliberately sets out to destroy the movement. This was not the case in Saskatchewan. Every successful model of co-operation in existence in Canada has been member-developed and member-driven.

The second negative lesson to be learned from the co-op farm experience is the danger of moving beyond the limits of the liberal-democratic Rochdale tradition in a country like Canada. Because co-op farms were an excursion beyond this tradition, they required extra internal resources. Sustaining a venture in co-operative community required charismatic leadership, powerful management, and business skills to succeed in the marketplace, and a high degree of ideological commitment. The movement lacked all three elements. There is no record of any significant personalities acknowledged as visionary leaders in the movement; the Federation of Production Co-operatives often spoke of the need for its members to receive training in business skills such as accounting; and the limited ideological commitment was evident when one of the leading co-op farmers was denounced publicly by fellow co-op farmers for his involvement in the Peace Movement.[41]

State Support for Worker Co-ops

Until the 1970s the worker co-op movement was scattered and occasional.[42] But the commitment of certain provincial governments to the concept has led to their rapid escalation. In Québec, which has the largest number of worker co-ops in Canada, it was the election of the Parti Québécois in 1976 that set the ideological stage for growth,[43] just as the election of the CCF in 1944 set the stage for co-op farm growth. Similarly, in the mid-1980s the New Democrats of Manitoba instituted a small worker co-op program, which in a few years gave the province a dozen worker co-ops.[44] However, both of these programs have been vulnerable to changes of government. When the Liberals defeated the Parti Québécois, support for the worker co-op development groups was reduced, and with the election of the Conservatives in Manitoba in 1988, the future for worker co-op development in that province is uncertain.

This is not to say that non-social democratic governments are inherently opposed to worker co-ops. In Prince Edward Island the Liberal administration of Joe Ghiz seems to be genuinely interested in worker co-ops as a part of a community-economic-development strategy.[45] Nevertheless, that government's orientation is primarily toward private-sector rather than co-op development. In a system that can elect a new government every four years, a co-op movement closely aligned with a particular party or its policy initiatives can suffer.

The maintenance of a liberal-democratic identity is especially important to sustain ties to the established co-op movement in Canada. Although the established co-ops in Saskatchewan were initially positive toward co-op farming, it did not receive high priority because there was not a mass movement. In its 1949 position paper titled "The Place and Function of Co-operative Enterprise in a Socialistic Economy," the Co-operative Union of Saskatchewan featured a number of issues -- co-op farming was among the last.[46]

In the case of today's worker co-op movement, the support of the Co-operative Union of Canada (now the Canadian Co-operative Association) has been persistent ever since its 1984 task-force study called on the federal government to fund a worker co-op program.[47] In 1988 the Canadian Co-operative Association received a $250,000 Federal government Innovations grant to study worker buyouts. Nevertheless, the co-op system is primarily a source of moral support rather than a direct actor through organizational and financial support in the creation of worker co-ops. Because of the split between Québec and English Canada and the resulting dual voices of the co-op movement, worker co-ops face an uneven development unless there is a single federal program for the whole country. An uneven development could mean an uncertain future, and that uncertainty would turn the co-op system to other priorities.

Future Models for Worker Ownership in Agriculture

Any model of worker ownership, especially a co-operative one that would arise in the agricultural sector, must take into account the historic trends that have marked agricultural development since the Second World War, that is, ever-larger units of production and less labour. Co-op farming cannot be given a mandate of repopulating a depleted rural society or rebuilding communities that have been destroyed by the marketplace, technological change, and urbanization. Its mandate must reflect these developments rather than struggle against them.

In Western Canada, where co-op farms came into being, the

factory-like operations of California agri-business do not exist. Instead the norm is the family-operated large-scale production unit with occasional seasonal help. With an ever-diminishing part of the gross domestic product and a workforce that is approaching five per cent, farming does not hold the promise of employment for many.[48] It is an industry for the few. Worker ownership using the co-operative model would have to be different in today's economy. The concept of farming co-operatives or of production co-ops in agriculture does, nevertheless, fit the trend toward larger and larger units of production. Large-scale farming would fit a worker co-op model. A worker co-op with a dozen members could farm 20,000 acres and it would still have the membership size of the earlier co-op farms.

Secondly, the continued bankruptcy of farmers provides a pool of recruits for co-operative farming ventures. Currently, government agencies that foreclose on farmers are willing to lease the land back to them. This could be done for a co-op operation as well.

Thirdly, the small business model of enterprise that is the norm for worker co-ops in Canada is already established in agriculture, where the producer is viewed as a small businessperson with an incorporated company.

For these factors to come into play, there must be deviations from the historical model created by co-op farms in Saskatchewan. First, the community-life aspects of the early co-op farms must be considered an option rather than an essential feature. Should the co-op farmer wish to reside in a town and commute to work, this possibility should be accepted. Second, the vagaries of agricultural production and commodity prices are such that farm production on its own is insufficient to guarantee economic viability for a worker co-op in agriculture. The new co-op farmer must give up the rigid division between worker and farmer that has existed traditionally and be prepared to create an agro-industrial business.

Finally, the issue of land ownership and land cost should be removed from co-op farming. The upfront capitalization presently required to start up in farming is prohibitive. Only with the existence of special programs that provide land on a long-term lease basis will co-operative farming be economically viable. The free land made available to veterans and the Saskatchewan Land Bank are examples of the importance of special programs in this sector of the economy.

Even with these reforms, a future worker co-op movement in agriculture will require a process of legitimization through some recognized and respected second party such as government, church, or labour. It will also require financial, legislative, and regulatory support both in the start-up phase and during periods of crisis. But the main factor in the building of a new model of co-op farming is how economically attractive it is to its potential membership. When farmers flocked by the thousands to the Wheat Pools they were lured by the promise and hope of increased prices for their grain; or when they created marketing co-ops for dairy products, they were interested in profit; and when the veterans decided to answer the call of the CCF government to form co-op farms they were offered the promise of crown land and grants. Involvement in the co-ops has always resulted from an economic carrot. Only a model that offers real and substantive benefits can hope to survive.

At present the factors that would support co-op farming do not exist. With the exception of the forestry sector,[49] the worker co-op model is currently on the edge of agriculture but has not yet penetrated it. The experience of co-op farming in Saskatchewan cannot help but spark interest in the past and reflections on future possibilities. Should the worker co-op sector become a significant reality in Canada, then there is no doubt that it would welcome an expansion into agricultural production. When that occurs, the co-op farms of Saskatchewan will not be forgotten.

Notes

[1] A. Nikiforuk, Sheila Pratt, and Don Wanagas, *Running on Empty: Alberta after the Boom* (Edmonton: NuWest Press, 1987), pp. 51-53, lists 954 farmers under the age of 35 as giving up farming between 1981 and 1986 out of a total of 40,000 in Alberta. About 350 farmers become bankrupt in the province annually.

[2]*Calgary Herald*, March 11, 1987, Section F.

[3]Ian MacPherson, *Each for All: A History of the Co-operative Movement in English Canada: 1900-1945* (Toronto: Macmillan, 1979), p. 16.

[4]Saskatchewan has maintained the highest rate of co-op membership per capita in Canada over a number of years. *Patterns and Trends of Canadian Co-operative Development* (Saskatoon: Co-operative College of Canada, 1982), p. 105, gives a figure of 45 per cent of Saskatchewan residents belonging to credit unions alone. The Saskatchewan Wheat Pool enrols a majority of the province's grain farmers and is the single largest non-government corporate entity in the province with sales of $1.8 billion in 1987.

[5]Gerald Friesen, *The Canadian Prairies: A History* (Toronto: University of Toronto Press, 1987), p. 409.

[6]S.M. Lipset, *Agrarian Socialism: The Co-operative Commonwealth Federation in Saskatchewan* (Berkeley: University of California Press, 1971), p. 332.

[7]Lois Ross, *Prairie Lives: The Changing Face of Farming* (Toronto: Between the Lines Press, 1984), p. 116.

[8]See G. Melnyk, *The Search for Community: From Utopia to a Co-operative Society* (Montré: Black Rose Books, 1985) for a more detailed explanation, page 15 on.

[9]For an analysis of the CCF's role in founding co-op farms see G. Melnyk, "The C.C.F. and the Establishment of Co-operative Farms in Saskatchewan: 1944-1952," in *The Theory and Practice of Co-operative Property*, ed. Jo-Anne Andre and David Laycock (Saskatoon: Canadian Association for Studies in Co-operation, 1987), pp. 111-123.

[10]L. Dietrick, *Matador: The Memoirs of a Co-operative Farmer*, unpublished manuscript courtesy of the author, pp. 34-35.

[11]L. Dietrick, *Matador*, p. 39.

[12]Jim Wright, *Co-operative Farming in Saskatchewan* (Regina: Government of Saskatchewan Bureau of Publications, 1949). Available at the Saskatchewan Archives Board, Regina, file of Department of Co-operation and Co-operative Development.

[13]Saskatchewan Archives Board, *T.C. Douglas Papers* (Report to the Cabinet Planning Board Conference), Executive Assistant's File 72, November 22, 1949.

[14]The farm population stood at 399,473 in 1951. (Figures presented at the Agricultural Production Co-operatives in Saskatchewan

Conference, April 13-14, 1964, sponsored by the Co-operative Union of Saskatchewan.)

[15]Saskatchewan Department of Co-operation and Co-operative Development, "Annual Report, 1949," p. E.S.7.

[16]Saskatchewan Department of Co-operation and Co-operative Development, "Annual Report, 1949," and the Agricultural Production Co-ops' Conference, 1964.

[17]Henry Cooperstock, "Prior Socialization and Co-operative Farming," in *Canadian Society*, ed. B. Blishen *et al.* (Toronto: Macmillan, 1964) pp. 227-228.

[18]*Family Herald*, February, 1958.

[19]Dennis Gruending, "Challenge at Matador," *Saskatoon Star-Phoenix*, August 31, 1972, p. 4.

[20]Henrik F. Infield, *Sociometric Structure of Veteran's Co-operative Land Settlement*, Sociometry Monograph 15 (New York: Beacon House, 1947), p. 15.

[21]Saskatchewan Archives Board, "Annual Report (1950) of the Department of Co-operation and Co-operative Development," p. E.S.5.

[22]"Agricultural Co-operatives in Saskatchewan: 1977 Directory," Department of Co-operation and Co-operative Development. Courtesy L. Dietrick.

[23]Letter of L.E. Dietrick to H.E. Chapman, Director of Extension Services Department of Co-operation and Co-operative Development, January 22, 1948. Courtesy of L. Dietrick.

[24]"Report of the Co-operative Farm Conference," Saskatoon, Dec. 1 & 2, 1949, p. 10. Courtesy of L. Dietrick.

[25]"Agricultural Production Co-ops in Saskatchewan" Conference Proceedings, Co-operative Union of Saskatchewan, p. 13.

[26]G.L. Fairbarin, *From Prairie Roots: The Remarkable Story of the Saskatchewan Wheat Pool* (Saskatoon: Western Producer Prairie Books, 1984), pp. 31-40.

[27]Saskatchewan Archives Board, *T.C. Douglas Papers* (Report to the Cabinet Planning Conference), Executive Assistant's File 72, November 22, 1949.

[28]"Report of the Co-operative Farm Conference," 1949, p. 11, and R. Jackall and Henry M. Levin, eds., *Worker Co-operatives in America* (Berkeley: University of California Press, 1984), p. 283.

[29]Brief by Victor Hay, n.d. Courtesy of L. Dietrick, Matador, Sask.

[30]*Saskatoon Star-Phoenix*, n.d.

[31]Ross, *Prairie Lives*, p. 116.

[32]Hutterites are a large religious sect located on farm colonies in Western Canada. These figures are taken from Alberta Report, January 18, 1988, p. 20.

[33]*Globe and Mail*, November 10, 1986, p. B5. The Hutterite colonies produce about a third of Manitoba's hogs. The plant had to be bailed out by Fletchers, a firm owned by Alberta and Saskatchewan hog producers, only two years later. *Globe and Mail*, March 7, 1988, p. B11.

[34]The details are available in G. Melnyk, "The C.C.F. and the Establishment of Co-op Farms," pp. 111-123.

[35]Figures provided at the Agricultural Production Co-ops Conference Proceedings, 1964, Co-operative Union of Saskatchewan.

[36]Gerald Friesen, "The Prairie West Since 1945: An Historical Survey," in *The Making of the Modern West: Western Canada Since 1945*, ed. A. W. Rasporich (Calgary, University of Calgary Press, 1984), p. 27.

[37]Nikiforuk, *Running on Empty*, p. 51.

[38]Economic Council of Canada, *Western Transitions* (Ottawa: Canadian Government Publication Centre, 1984), p. 82

[39]Ian MacPherson, "The CCF and the Co-operative Movement in the Douglas Years: An Uneasy Alliance," in *Building the Co-operative Commonwealth: Essays on the Democratic Socialist Tradition in Canada* ed. J. W. Brennan (Regina: Canadian Plains Research Centre, 1984), pp. 181-205.

[40]Mark Goldblatt, "Founding a Worker Co-op Sector: Lessons from Co-op Housing," *Worker Co-op*, 7 No. 4 (1988), 11.

[41]See L. Dietrick, *Matador*, p. 82.

[42]Ian MacPherson, "Reflections on the Uneven History of Worker Co-operatives in Canada," *Worker Co-op*, 6, No. 4 (1987), 8-11.

[43]B. Levesque *et al.*, *Profil Socio-Économique des Co-opératives de Travail au Québec* (Montréal: Université de Québec, 1985) state that of the 200 worker co-ops in Québec, 85 per cent had been established since 1970 and 52 per cent since 1980. The Parti Québecois government amended the Co-operatives Act in 1984 to serve more clearly worker co-ops. It made money available for loans to worker co-ops and also financed resource groups that aided the development of

worker co-operatives. (See "Québec Pledges $8 Million for Worker Co-operatives," *Worker Co-op*, 4, No. 4 (1985).

[44]Jeremy Hull indicates that by 1988, the year the NDP was defeated as the government of Manitoba, that "30 worker co-operatives had been incorporated. Many of these have not yet become operational." *Worker Co-op*, 8, No. 1 (1988), 12.

[45]"Interview with Leonce Bernard, P.E.I.'s Minister of Industry," *Worker Co-op*, 7, No. 3 (1988), p. 11.

[46]Saskatchewan Archives Board, *T.C. Douglas Papers* (Co-operative Union of Saskatchewan's Brief to the Government on the Place and Function of Co-operative Enterprise in a Socialistic Economy), Premier's File 106, January 12, 1949.

[47]*A Co-operative Development Strategy for Canada* (Ottawa: Co-operative Union of Canada, 1984).

[48]Economic Council, *Western Transition*, p. 73.

[49]See "Québec's Forestry Co-operatives: A Major Success Story," *Worker Co-op*, 6, No.1 (1986).

Chapter 5

The Multi-Stakeholder Approach to Worker Ownership

John E. Jordan[1]

A Rationale for a Multi-Stakeholder Concept of Organization

Despite the resurgence of interest in various forms of economic democracy, few would contend that we have an extensive repertoire of effective models. A few years ago The Co-operators Group, a holding company for The Co-operators insurance and other enterprises,[2] began a fundamental search for more effective organizational models. The result is "the multi-stakeholder co-operative," the first of which began operations in 1987. This chapter analyzes the multi-stakeholder and comments on its relevance for proponents of worker ownership.

The multi-stakeholder co-operative deals simultaneously with two common issues. First, while co-operatives at their origin were an immense advance in economic democratization, the customary form of co-operatives has the paradoxical effect of excluding some interested parties. Second, there is frequently a mismatch between the membership and control base of a co-operative and the groups that have fundamental interests in it; this mismatch often leads to performance difficulties and contributes to the declining role of co-operatives in many sectors. I will explore these issues in more detail.

At the time of their rise in the nineteenth and early twentieth century, co-operatives represented the extension of democracy into economic life. Members were enfranchised and empowered to determine how their socio-economic needs were to be met. For a movement that was interested in expanding democracy, there is, however, one peculiarity. Each co-operative is defined around only one of its possible membership bases. In effect, it is a single stakeholder organization. Thus, there are co-operatives of consumers or workers or primary producers. The effect is to include one group while excluding other groups who have a significant interest. The resulting problems periodically lead to efforts to deal with the "relationships" between, for example, farmer producer co-operatives and consumer co-operatives. But there have been few efforts to rethink the organizational logic that is the basis of the problem.

The second issue is two-dimensional. One aspect is the view that a mismatch between the conventional structure of co-operatives and the parties with fundamental interests in them is responsible for the current decline of co-operatives in many sectors and countries. Most co-operatives are formed to meet pressing needs of the particular constituency or interest group that forms the membership base. But over time other interests usually come into play. The co-operative hires a staff who become an interest. If the co-operative relies significantly on external financing, the investors become an interest. If it is a producer co-operative with longstanding, stable relations with purchasers, they become an interest. These interests are not represented in the membership or at the board table, but particularly if the co-operative experiences difficulty, their significance quickly becomes clear. It is misleading, however, to see these interests as becoming real only *in extremis*; rather it is these situations that enable us to recognize the fundamental forces and interests.

One recent example is the re-organization proposal of the Berkeley, California consumer co-operative into a hybrid consumer-worker co-operative after a period of persistent operating losses. Another would be the role of lenders or financiers, be they co-operative financial institutions or others, when the borrower encounters difficulty. In the case of a Canadian farm machinery co-operative, the farmers were the only members, and they took far less interest in trying to re-organize the co-operative than did the lenders, who felt they had more at stake.

The mismatch is particularly apparent in consumer co-operatives where the member's financial stake is often very small, for example, five dollars has been the norm in Canadian credit unions, and less than one hundred dollars is typical in many consumer co-operatives. Consumers tend to be transient, especially when the retail and banking sectors are intensely competitive, and thus the need for a co-operative presence in these sectors is less obvious. Can a membership with little at stake financially or psychologically provide the solid, coherent direction that any enterprise needs in order to survive in a turbulent and competitive environment? Is it surprising that many such co-operatives tend to be rudderless? The formal base of the organization, the membership, takes only a passing interest in them. As a result, the organization falls more under the sway of management, and a small self-selected segment of the membership. The broader interest of the staff or other parties is not represented in the formal decision process.

At times the mismatch assumes highly questionable proportions. In Britain, for example, it was shown a decade ago that the employees had more invested in the consumer co-operatives than did the members, due to the practice of re-investing employee pension funds in the co-operatives. Quite aside from the pension fund investments, it should be apparent that employees are significant stakeholders. But here even with the fund investments, the employees were in most cases severely limited in their right of participation, and in no case acknowledged as a distinct interest, except in by-laws that restricted employee board representation to a small, set number.[3] Alex Laidlaw gave a parable which suggests how illogical this is in the case of producer co-operatives as well:

> Imagine two brothers, one a fisherman, and the other a skilled worker in a co-op fish plant. One goes to sea, early in the

morning and returns with a load of fish. The workers in the
plant take over and complete the job -- filleting, packing or
canning, storing and preparing for market. Isn't the task a
continuous one from the time the fish is caught until it goes to
market? All hands are engaged in essentially the same effort.
The fishermen and plant workers are actually partners in the
same venture. The plant workers are not incidental to the the
operation but full-time participants. They are a vital part of
the whole enterprise and they have a stake in its success as
well as the fishermen; and by what logic are they excluded
from the [membership and] Board?

Similarly, co-operative theory and practice have presented
the relationship between the local co-operative and secondary
federations or associations as one-directional; the locals form the
membership and board of the secondary organization. This
overlooks the extensive interest that the secondary has in the
local, to which it is a significant supplier of goods, services,
financing, etc. Because this relationship is not acknowledged and
reflected in the control structure, it is played out at the
managerial level where the nature of the interest is likely to be
masked.

The decline in consumer retail co-operation in a great many
countries can be explained in large measure by the mismatch
between the formal membership base of the co-operative and the
real interest groups in it. In a sense it is the co-operative version
of the Berle and Means thesis;[4] co-operatives with a broad
membership, but with only few members having a significant
stake, will not be responsive to their members or to other
significant parties. And as the current corporate raiders argue,
organizations without a legitimate constituency giving clear
direction tend to perform poorly over time.[5]

Kurt Lewin's concept of lifespace is useful in identifying the
interests which can form the base for a solid membership
structure in a co-operative.[6] According to Lewin, we can graph
our life by indicating the relative proportions that are taken up
by shopping, working, family activity, etc. One can use time,
expenditure, or some other variable as an index. It is unlikely
that lifespace can be systematized into a rigorous instrument, but
it can be of great heuristic value in designing co-operatives. It
also helps to explain why housing and childcare co-operatives

tend to be more successful consumer co-operatives than retail ones, and why farmer producer co-operatives tend to be more successful than consumer retail co-operatives. In each case, the successful co-operatives tend to be those whose business occupies a large portion of the lifespace of their members. In short, the formal structure and membership base of the co-operative is congruent with the nature of the significant interests in it. If one graphs the lifespace of the co-operative, it can enable the identification of interests that are central but which may not now be represented.

The dominant tradition of single stakeholder co-operatives should not obscure a persistent search for a more inclusive model. A key struggle took place around the formation of the International Co-operative Alliance (ICA) in 1895. The French and some others on the continent argued that the practice of "co-partnership" should be adopted as a requirement for ICA membership. Their concern was that the conventional consumer or producer co-operative did not adequately recognize the rights and contributions of the co-operative's employees. Co-partnership was eventually defeated due to a changing mix of delegates and the influence of the Fabians, who argued that the state of being a consumer was common to everyone and thus a universal basis for co-operative membership. As in any other enterprise, the interests of the employees in a co-operative should be met through trade unions.[7] This holds today as the conventional wisdom in most co-operatives.

There has been small but continuous interest in alternate forms of co-ownership or co-partnership. Many have noted that Eroski, the retail co-operative in Mondragon is organized with a dual membership base of workers and consumers so that the interests of each are recognized. As in Berkeley, some conventional consumer co-operatives in other countries have resorted to enfranchising staff in efforts to overcome severe difficulties. But these still remain exceptions and are often referred to as "hybrid co-operatives," the very name indicating their ambiguous heritage.

The argument so far is that co-operatives are best composed of the various groups which have a real, sustained, and fundamental interest in them. This is because organizations perform better when they are owned and governed by interest groups. They do not do well when they are run on behalf of an absentee-owner, regardless of whether we call that absentee-owner a small shareholder, a co-operative member, a government, or the public. But it is not simply a question of pragmatics. It is also a normative question of what is right. Who should benefit from the success of a co-operative? Who should bear the risk of loss? Who should determine the direction the co-operative takes?

If one surveys how this question has been addressed in other forms of organization, there tends to be a common thread in the positions taken: A single exclusive interest should be dominant. Thus, for example, the conventional consumer and producer co-operative tradition relies fundamentally on the logic of the primacy of use. This logic has a tradition in law extending back to the Roman concept of the *jus fructi*. Under it, users are entitled to the benefit. By contrast, worker co-operative advocates often justify their claims by reference to the labour theory of value; the surplus is created exclusively by the efforts of the workers, and they alone are entitled to it. Some co-operators and most capitalists believe it is capital which is the generative force in enterprises and should thus be solely credited with the resulting rewards.

In considering these opposing claims, one might well ask why each must be exclusive. After all, consumers (especially corporate consumers) often contribute extensively to product development which benefits the supplier. How, on the other hand, can user-owners of a consumer co-operative see the contribution of staff only *in extremis*? And in a market or mixed economy, how can users and staff not see that some investors make a legitimate contribution to the success of an organization? The position taken here is that the various parties with major interests in an organization should have the right to have their stakeholder status legitimated.

The question then is, can we redefine the organization so that it is a product of the various interests that contribute to its effectiveness? Can we acknowledge the legitimacy of multiple and even opposing interests? Can we design an organization that specifies the nature of the different interests and allocates them an appropriate role? This is what the multi-stakeholder organization or multi-stakeholder co-operative attempts to do.

The language of "stakeholders" has acquired currency over the past decade as a way of recognizing and legitimizing a broader degree of interest in organizations. The appointment of directors from minorities on corporate boards is one manifestation. Generally, though, "stakeholder" is taken as a metaphor rather than as a legitimate interest with entailed rights. More cynically, some use it to identify those interests a corporation should be wary of because they could interfere with the corporation's plans and strategies. Reflecting this view, stakeholder assumption analysis has become a tool in corporate planning.[8] On the other hand, what would result if one took the concept of stakeholder seriously and applied it rigorously to the design of a co-operative?

The Legal Structure

For this we need a different concept of the corporation. The theory which acknowledges the corporation to be a legal person creates yet another interest, that of the body corporate itself. The corporation becomes reified, and actions are undertaken in the name of "the corporate good" without it being clear in which stakeholders' interest this may or may not be. There is another way to think about corporations. As Ackoff puts it:

> The appropriate objective of a corporation conceptualized as an organization . . . is *not* to serve any of its stakeholders groups to the exclusion of any of the others. *It is to serve all of them by increasing their ability to pursue their objectives more efficiently and effectively.* This corporate objective seems to imply that a corporation should have no purpose of its own. It should be no more than an instrument of others. . . .Serving stakeholders should be a purpose of a corporation. . . .It views the corporation as an instrument of *all* its stakeholders.[9]

In other words, a corporation may be a legal person, but it should not be seen as a person that is independent or autonomous in its interests. Its interests are those of its stakeholders. It has none of its own.

This view of the corporation is akin to the agency concept of corporation, which is recognized in corporate and tax law as basically a pass-through form for the parties with a beneficial interest. One looks to them on questions of intentionality and purpose, and for fundamental responsibility of the agent-entity. This concept of a corporation, more than the concept of the corporation as an autonomous person, is closer to what we need as a basis for a multi-stakeholder co-operative.

What then is a stakeholder? It is first of all important to get the perspective correct. The stakeholder logic is designed to empower defined interests; this means that a stakeholder is defined by the organization's importance to the stakeholder and not vice versa. For example, an organization could not argue that employees are not stakeholders because the unemployment rate is high and the labour pool is plentiful. Rather, if employees are heavily dependent on the organization, they are entitled to stakeholder status.

Therefore, we must go beyond a generic definition of stakeholder as an organized interest which is significantly affected by the action or inaction of an organization. The breadth of this definition also poses difficulties; it is so broad that it would include, for example, competitors that one would not want to empower. This definition also suggests that the stakeholders are passive parties who simply receive the organization's actions. Instead, we want a definition that sees the organization as the product of the stakeholder's purposes and activity. For these reasons, a more appropriate definition of stakeholders is: those organized interests who co-produce the results of the organization.

An analysis of operating companies within The Co-operators Group revealed that several interests were constant: the users of services, the providers of services (staff), and The Co-operators Group. We looked at broader interests such as the community and concluded that it was difficult to define the appropriate relationship. As a result, we began with relationships that were clear, while keeping open the possibility of extending the model at a later point.

In many situations the user is not an obvious stakeholder.

The co-operative may not matter significantly to some users of its services. Whether it does or not may depend both upon the nature of the business relationship and on the value that the user puts on being part of a co-operative. One can illustrate from two different Co-operators companies. One is Co-operators Data Services Limited, which provides an extensive range of computer services to credit unions, insurance companies, and other financial institutions. The performance of Co-operators Data is critical to its clients' well-being because it maintains all of their account information. It has long-term contracts with its clients and serves them daily. The other example is Co-operators Communications Limited which provides media services to businesses. In contrast to CDSL, most of its work is on a project basis. It will do one project for a client and then may not have another request for months. Its business relationship is generally episodic, yet some clients want to be involved as stakeholders either because of the importance of the service or because they prefer that kind of relationship with a supplier. So although we see users as a category which should have the option of becoming stakeholders, the likelihood of that happening will vary considerably. In all cases, we have established criteria for user or client stakeholders, including a minimum amount of business per year and a commitment not to compete with the co-operative.

Staff seems to be a clearcut category, but we have found that they do not all see it that way. Younger, more mobile staff may not see themselves as having the long-term interest in the organization that is implied in the stakeholder model.

The Co-operators Group provides the entrepreneurial initiative and usually supplies the initial capital for new companies. It also provides a link with the broader co-operative community and sees that there is desirable co-ordination among Co-operators companies.[10]

In a conventional corporate setting, these three groups would represent customers, labour, and capital. But that means that their interests are opposing. How can they be brought together in one organization? The difference in interests is real and cannot be masked. But the question is whether the three groups can see that their interests-in-common outweigh their particular interests. This perception of common interests is the starting point of the multi-stakeholder model. Thus, the multi-stakeholder model developed by The Co-operators is designed to empower each of the three stakeholder interests, and to address the issues identified above.

A Multi-Stakeholder Organization Model and Three Pilots

The argument thus far only articulates why a multi-stakeholder form is desirable and specifies who the primary stakeholder groups should be. One now faces a considerable design challenge. What form should stakeholder participation take? How are three different interests to be positively related in an organization? How will the potential of conflict be addressed? What should be the balance between the three interests?

We approached these issues by setting out the principles which would act as a framework for the design of specific multi-stakeholder co-operatives. The policy incorporating these principles and authorizing the implementation of a few pilots was given board approval in August 1985. Design committees were then established to develop specific models for each organization which took into account the financial and other business requirements, stakeholder views and preferences, and legal and tax implications. Because much of that work was necessarily technical, this analysis will focus on the principles, while illustrating them with examples from the three pilots: Co-operators Data Services Limited (CDSL), Co-operators Development Corporation Limited (CDCL, property development and management), and Co-operators Communications Limited (CCL, media and video services). These principles were grouped into three headings.

Commitment and Balance

First of all, it is important that there be a commitment to being a stakeholder. This means that involvement must be voluntary. One cannot be compelled to be a stakeholder. We express this by saying stakeholder status is an option or opportunity; it is not a given. To activate the option, the stakeholders must agree upon their expectations of each other, themselves, and the organization and make a commitment to follow through on their respective responsibilities. Part of the stakeholder commitment is to help other stakeholders achieve their goals; stakeholding extends beyond protecting self-interest. Rather, it is a new enactment of mutual self-help. Commitment leads to a positive result from groups whose interests may be partly in opposition.

But beyond a commitment to each other, the groups must establish a structure which makes positive interaction possible and even likely. We express this in a principle of balance between the different stakeholder groups. Some parts of this are relatively clear. For example, it was readily agreed that no one group should have an absolute majority on a board, but this still left room for considerable discussion as to what the relative weighting should be. Does balance mean that each group should have one-third? Or should one group be given a clear lead-role? If so, which group? As the chart below indicates, one technique used to provide overall balance was to allocate a leading position to different groups on different dimensions. This was not a conscious part of the original design, but as each issue was addressed on its own merits, it turned out that this pattern evolved. We also dealt with balance within each stakeholder group. Client voting rights and equity participation are set according to a formula which recognizes the diversity of client size and its use of services. Similarly there is a formula for staff, but in this case it sets out that all staff will purchase the same number of voting shares (five) and about the same amount of equity shares (this amount is pegged to the average annual salary so it will change over time). Enacting the stakeholder option means entering into a membership agreement which includes these provisions and other rights and responsibilities. This means there is a defined structure to stakeholding, which helps to maintain overall balance.

Voice and Representation

Stakeholders should have a voice and a vote. We draw on Hirschman's voice concept to make clear that it is not only a question of a periodic vote but also of a regular voice.[11] It is also important to ensure that each stakeholder group can elect its own representatives, such as delegates or directors, rather than having them chosen by an election at large.

On issues other than elections, general meeting decisions which require votes are made by counting votes held by all stakeholder groups. But here one encounters the balance question again. If each stakeholder has a voting share, then the votes accruing to each group will vary with the number of members at any given point. This would make the balance unpredictable and precarious. We allocated voting rights to each group on a stable basis, so they will not fluctuate with each year's financial results or the admission of new members in one stakeholder group. This is done by creating three classes of members and allocating to each class a fixed percentage of the votes in a general meeting (see Table 5.1). The percentage of votes does not change regardless of the number of members admitted or shares issued, or represented at the meeting (as long as the quorum requirement is met). Thus, voting rights for stakeholder groups in general meetings would not be determined by precisely how much capital a stakeholder or a stakeholder group has. It also has the peculiar result that a member's vote is a shifting fraction of the total votes depending on the number of members (voting) in a class.

We also decided that the general manager and members of the management group are not eligible for election to the board of their multi-stakeholder co-operative. They can be staff stakeholders but not directors. We wanted to make clear that the intent was to enfranchise staff generally not to give additional voice to management.

Table 5.1

Allocation of Votes to Stakeholders

	The Group	Clients	Staff
Data Services			
Directors	4	4	4
% AGM votes	51	29	20
Development			
Directors	3	2	2
% AGM votes	100	tbd	tbd
Communications			
Directors	2	2	2
% AGM votes	51	20	29

Note. AGM = Annual General Meeting;
     tdb = to be determined.

Financial

The financial dimension was even more complex to understand and design. One question was the extent to which stakeholders should participate in capitalizing the organization and sharing in the financial results. The federal co-operatives' act imposed some constraints by requiring that shares be issued and redeemed only at par value.

There was early agreement on broad principles. One is that stakeholders should participate fully in the financial dimension of the co-operative. This means the responsibility to raise capital and to share both gains and losses and the net worth of the co-operative if it is successful. Each stakeholder is expected to subscribe for shares, and the required investment must be significant and formula-based. The amount is not a question of individual choice once the decision has been to enact one's stakeholder status. In the case of Co-operators Data, clients subscribe for shares equal to 15 per cent of their annual billings by CDSL; staff subscribe for shares equal to 15 per cent of the average annual salary at the time that they join. In both cases, share purchases can be paid over several years through payroll deduction for staff and by an addition to monthly billings for clients.

Profit or surplus distribution was more difficult. How much should be allocated to each stakeholder group? And how could a stakeholder receive its share? Co-operators Data and the other companies are capital-intensive businesses. CDSL requires almost one dollar in assets to support one dollar of revenue. It needs to retain as much of its earnings as possible to enable its asset growth to support growth in services and revenue. If it paid out its profits, it would be weaker. Yet stakeholders could not benefit from notional participation in a growing pool of retained earnings through increased share value, as would be the normal case in a joint-stock company, because co-op shares cannot increase beyond their par value.

This problem was resolved by setting up a capital account for each stakeholder. The capital account idea was influenced by the Mondragon practice. Each year, a fair return on shares purchased and the stakeholder's share of the remaining annual profit (stakeholder surplus participation or SSP) is allocated to its capital account. This capital account remains part of the retained earnings of Co-operators Data and is at risk of future loss. If there is a loss in a year, half of it would be set against the corporate reserve and half against the capital accounts. Dividends to members are paid out of the capital accounts.

There is a predetermined order in which annual profits must be distributed. After provision for income taxes, required reserves are set aside and then a fair return is set on the shares purchased. (Provision has also been made for the issuance of preferred shares which could be purchased by non-members, although none has been issued as yet. These would rank ahead of the stakeholder equity shares in right to a return.) Any remaining balance is distributed to stakeholders as stakeholder surplus participation (SSP). The intent is that the allocation to each class of members would reflect the respective contribution to the creation of the annual earnings. Because this requires board discretion, broad bands were set in the by-laws within which the board can decide.

Table 5.2

Stakeholder Surplus Participation (SSP)

	Data Services % of Total SSP	Communications % of Total SSP
The Group	5-20	20-60
Clients	35-60	20-60
Staff	35-60	20-60

The allocation to the Clients group would be divided among the clients pro rata according to their volume of business. Data company staff debated at length how their SSP would be divided, and several formulas were developed. In the end, it was decided to distribute equally to all staff stakeholders.

Thus a member's financial stake consists of three elements:

- voting shares (determined by a formula, and not financially significant);

- equity shares (determined by a formula); and

- capital account (containing amounts allocated for fair return on equity shares purchased, for rent of funds in the account over the previous year, and for stakeholder surplus participation).

In this manner we have struck a balance between enabling

Co-operators Data to retain its earnings to fund future growth and enabling stakeholders to share in the growing increase in the net worth of the organization. At the same time, because this approach is based on book value, it avoids potential speculative market values for the organization and thus respects co-operative principles.

The Results so Far

Both clients and staff have responded favourably to the introduction of the multi-stakeholder model. The most fully developed model is in CDSL which is also the oldest and largest company. About one-third of its 700 staff have exercised their option. Based on the eligible staff, the participation rate is somewhat higher. Clients representing about two-thirds of CDSL business volume have exercised their stakeholder option and subscribed over $2.7 million in share capital in the initial year.

Based on the operating results for 1987 and 1988, the board allocated an eight per cent fair return on equity shares, and on amounts in the capital accounts. The SSP was allocated as follows: the Group (5%); Clients (44%); and Staff (51%).

These amounts were allocated to each stakeholder's capital account. Each year, the board also declared cash dividends of $500,000, which were payable out of the capital accounts.

Co-operators Development also had a positive response to its initial year. Its program is structured quite differently. Simply put, about 70 per cent of the staff have exercised their option (the capital requirement is considerably lower than CDSL's), and both major clients are participating. They too had a significant allocation on the basis of CDCL's first year's results.

Co-operators Communications is just introducing its multi-stakeholder program. In this case the staff numbers only eight, and all are expected to participate. Major clients are now being approached, and already three have indicated an intention to join.

It is still far too early to draw any definitive conclusions from the experience to date, but the feedback from participants indicates that they do feel more involved in the co-operative and take a greater interest in its affairs. It is through this cementing of interests that the co-operative can be effective in its role of helping all its stakeholders achieve their goals.

Implications

What are the implications of the multi-stakeholder model for advancing the cause of worker-ownership? First, the model is a means of bringing a significant measure of worker-ownership into existing base co-operatives and other enterprises. Limited, but not token, forms are important ways to introduce both workers and other constituencies to the reality (as against the idea) of worker-ownership. Existing organizations are far more ready to support worker co-operatives if the former have had direct experience of even limited participation in worker-ownership.

In the late-1970s, when The Co-operators was requested to participate in financing a worker buyout of a Peterborough chainsaw plant, there was little understanding of or experience with worker-ownership. The multi-stakeholder co-operatives have changed this considerably, and made it possible to gain the participation of The Co-operators in the financial package prepared for the Canadian Porcelain project. An important strategy for advancing worker ownership is to seek out situations where partial worker-ownership can be achieved, particularly situations which recognize both the democratic and financial aspects of ownership.

Second, the experience of different models will help us to determine what models of worker-ownership are well-adopted to the Canadian environment. In the United States, there is a greater willingness to use ESOPs and other less than ideal forms to establish worker-ownership. Our lack of significant experience with varied models should encourage us to be experimental, too.

Finally, much of the preceding argument has been that enterprise ownership only by workers may not be the height of economic democracy or fulfill the requirements of natural justice. Models like the multi-stakeholder one will help us to develop a more balanced approach to achieving economic democracy which recognizes the legitimate aspirations of different constituencies.

Notes

[1]This paper is based on a several-year process of designing and introducing multi-stakeholder co-operatives in The Co-operators Group Limited. This process involved a number of colleagues from whom I learned and who will find some of their views expressed in this paper: Teunis Haalboom, Peter Hlushko, Ralph Ulmer, Dennis Deters, Joe Martin, Maggi Rankin, Karl Wettstein, Tymen Donkersgoed, Rev. J.J. MacDonald, Warren Hanstead, and Lorne Motton. I also want to thank my mentors who will detect their influence: Russ Ackoff, Eric Trist, Trevor Williams; and extend my appreciation to Gordon Farquharson, who brought creativity and rigor to the challenges involved in grounding in law a new corporate form.

[2]What is now The Co-operators Group Limited began in the mid-1940s as co-operative leaders in Saskatchewan and Ontario each established co-operative insurers. These were brought together as The Co-operators in 1976. The Co-operators Group Limited is incorporated under the federal Co-operatives Act. Its 35 member-owners are provincial, regional, and national co-operatives from all major sectors (grain handling, dairies, wholesalers, housing, credit-union centrals, and others) across Canada. The Group in turn owns a series of operating companies, including Canada's largest general insurance company, a life insurance company, several other insurance operations, as well as four new enterprises, three of which have been established as multi-stakeholder co-operatives.

[3]See G. N. Ostergaard and A. H. Halsey, *Power in Co-operatives: A Study of Democratic Control in British Retail Societies* (Oxford: Basil Blackwell, 1965) for the background to this issue. In 1980, Alex Laidlaw showed me an article reporting on the extent of employee pension-fund investment in the retail co-operatives. P. Milford, "Worker Co-operatives and Consumer Co-operatives: Can They Be Combined?" in *Labour-owned Firms and Workers' Co-operatives*, ed. S. Jansson and A. B. Britt (London: Gower Publishing, 1986) claims it totals 60 per cent of the equity.

[4]A. Berle and G. Means, *The Modern Corporation and Private Property* (New York: Macmillan, 1932).

[5]The thesis has found new academic support in the shareholder value theory developed by Alfred Rappaport at Northwestern. See

A. Rappaport, "Selecting Strategies that Create Shareholder Value," *Harvard Business Review*, 59, 3 (1981), pp. 139-149.

[6]K. Lewin, *Field Theory in Social Science* (New York: Harper & Brothers, 1951).

[7]P. N. Backstrom, *Christian Socialism and Co-operation in Victorian England* (London: Croom Helm, 1974); W. P. Watkins, *The International Co-operative Alliance 1895-1970* (London: I.C.A., 1970); and Paul Derrick, *Co-ownership, Co-operation and Control: An Industrial Objective* (London: Longmans, 1969). Derrick remains a contemporary proponent of co-parternership.

[8]J. R. Emshoff, *Managerial Breakthroughs: Action Strategies for Strategic Change* (New York: AMACOM, 1980).

[9]R. L. Ackoff, *Creating the Corporate Future: Plan or be Planned For* (New York: John Wiley, 1981), pp. 33-34.

[10]J. E. Jordan, "A System of Interdependent Firms as a Development Strategy," in *Labour-owned Firms and Workers' Co-operatives*, ed. S. Jansson and A.B. Britt (London: Gower Publishing, 1986).

[11]A. D. Hirschman, *Exit, Voice and Loyalty* (Cambridge: Harvard University Press, 1970).

Chapter 6

Worker Co-operatives for Disabled Individuals

Judith Brown

The worker co-operative provides a flexible employment environment that can accommodate the special needs of disabled individuals. Application of the worker co-operative model in Europe demonstrates that disabled individuals can control their own workplace and function as productive members of society. After sketching some of the European literature, this chapter will provide a detailed analysis of a Canadian attempt to create a worker co-operative for the psychiatrically disabled. Subsequently, a development strategy for the disabled will be presented.

Worker Co-operatives -- An International Perspective

Several European nations have recognized that unemployment of their disabled citizens constitutes an important social rather than personal problem. Because employers seek the most skilled and the least disabled employees, the handicapped, often characterized by poor work histories due to illness-related absences, are the ones who are "last to be hired and first to be fired." Acknowledging the burdens that this practice imposes, several nations have developed programs such as quota systems,

132

job creation, and subsidized employment for those with physical and psychiatric disabilities.

The worker co-operative model is one such program. For example, in Poland, 436 co-operatives employing 200,000 disabled workers have been developed.[1] These co-ops were started when individuals who had been disabled in the Second World War were, by necessity, forced to share tools and expertise. Co-operatives for the disabled initially concentrated on labour-intensive endeavours such as shoe and furniture repairs. The subsequent demand for manufactured goods led to the industrialization and mechanization of production.[2] Worker co-operatives received public funds for construction and later expansion. Development was also facilitated through tax rebates and production monopolies. As a result, the co-operatives operated by disabled individuals have become highly successful businesses that provide members with competitive wages and benefits such as healthcare, pensions, vacation time, leisure facilities, and various rehabilitation and social services.[3]

The Europeans' strong commitment to work and their belief that every individual who desires employment should have a job have led to a perspective that is substantially different from that of the North American rehabilitation community. In Europe, workshops for the disabled are viewed as places of work not treatment settings; emphasis is placed on business operations rather than social services. As a result, disabled individuals in several European nations such as Poland, Hungary, Scandinavian countries, and the Netherlands have been restored to being productive members of their community.

Traditional Rehabilitation Programs

The North American system of rehabilitation has not demonstrated the same commitment to work as its European counterpart. Employment opportunities available to the disabled are primarily in sheltered workshops -- a heavily structured environment that combines counselling, recreation, and "vocational training." Theoretically, this combination of programs provides an opportunity for the disabled to develop the social and vocational skills that lead to employment in the regular business community.

Workshops have been criticized for emphasizing intrapsychic factors rather than real world experiences. Clients arrive at workshops with a label that shapes the staff's perception and focuses on the individual's dependence rather than capacities. Organized more as a clinic than a workplace, emphasis is placed on thoughts and feelings rather than upon productive labour.[4]

In sheltered workshops the disabled are a form of underclass that performs menial assembly-line tasks for as little as 70 to 90 cents per hour. Low wages diminish the value of work in the rehabilitation process and underline the point that productive work is secondary to psychotherapy. The token payment and the meaningless nature of the work also reduce the incentive to be productive and depress the client's self-esteem. Physically-disabled individuals, who are treated as having a greater degree of disability than is actually the case, perform below their capacity.[5] The acquired social and psychological factors surrounding the disability (e.g., through the interaction with the social workers) pose a greater obstacle to rehabilitation than the disability itself.[6] Despite the widespread availability of traditional rehabilitation programs, unemployment rates for the psychiatrically-disabled remain between 90 - 95 per cent.[7] Indeed Anthony and Blanch suggest that:

> The mental-health and rehabilitation system seems to have done a better job of teaching persons with psychiatric disabilities how to be clients than in teaching them how to be workers. At the time of hospital discharge, a person who is severely psychiatrically-disabled has a much better probability of returning to the hospital than of returning to work![8]

The ineffectiveness of the workshop model, revealed in these unemployment rates, led many dissatisfied clients and mental-health professionals to consider an alternative model.

Supported Employment

The supported-employment approach places severely disabled individuals into competitive employment (i.e., in the "regular" workplace beside workers who are not handicapped). Its goal is to increase employment opportunities for people with disabilities.

Several supported employment projects have demonstrated that individuals previously labeled "permanently unemployable" could, with ongoing assistance, perform successfully in competitive business environments. The model provides the disabled individual with the resources necessary to ensure job success. For example, the disabled employee often has a job coach who assists throughout the entire employment process. The coach assists in obtaining a position in the workforce, teaches the job to the client, mediates co-worker and employer relations, and addresses such non-work issues as transportation to the job site, accommodation, medication, etc. These programs reduce long-term public expenditures and improve the disabled person's self-image, confidence, level of functioning, and contribution to the community.[9]

Although supported employment has assisted many disabled workers to find jobs, severely psychiatrically-disabled individuals have difficulty locating work in the public and private sector. Negative stereotypes, poor work records, and medically-related absenteeism are an additional burden. In an effort to overcome the problems of supported employment for the psychiatrically disabled, some community workers in Canada and the United States are experimenting with the worker co-operative. One experiment that was recently attempted in Ontario is instructive because it points out many of the problems that must be solved before this approach to supported work can succeed.

Able Courier Limited

This courier service operated by psychiatrically-disabled workers represents a bold experiment in supported employment. In order to proceed with developing the business, a Community Development Corporation was established. The Board of Directors of the Community Development Corporation consisted of interested community members with experience in mental health, business, and community development. Two members of Able Courier were also on this Board.

This arrangement provided Able's employees with professional assistance in business matters. The Community Development Corporation was also used to obtain grant money for the co-operative, including funding for start-up capitalization.

Able Courier was subsequently incorporated as a share-capital corporation with the structure of a worker co-operative. The co-operative was governed by decisions made at quarterly general meetings in which each person would have one vote. The Board of Directors was elected by and responsible to the general membership. Management was elected at the general meeting for a term of two years. Membership was expanded or terminated by majority vote at a general meeting. New members were on probation for six months. Pay scales and job classification were under the control of the membership.

Able Courier required $45,000 in start-up capital for development and equipment. Traditional lending institutions expressed little interest in financing the venture. Funds for the project were eventually secured from two public sources and a private agency. Workers were not required to make any financial contribution.

After incorporating the Community Development Corporation and the Co-operative, and after creating the by-laws defining the relationship between the two structures, members of the Boards attended developmental workshops. They solicited members for the co-operative and hired a general manager with experience in both mental health and the courier business. On June 1, 1987, Able Courier Limited opened its doors for business. The business provided a variety of jobs including dispatchers, couriers, a receptionist, and a bookkeeper. Shifts and schedules were set up to accommodate workers' needs.

Financial Difficulties

Within the first year another $44,000 was required for operating costs. The financial difficulties resulted from unanticipated equipment expenditures and an exceedingly optimistic revenue forecast. These financial problems required Able's directors to return to the granting agencies for additional funding. Ministry officials made further funding contingent on dissolving the business' co-operative structure. The Ministry's proposal caused a great deal of conflict within the Board of Directors. After lengthy negotiations, the Board of Directors of the Community Development Corporation agreed to sacrifice Able's co-operative structure.

The business now operates under the direction of the Board of the Community Development Corporation. While the workers' representation on the Board of the Community Development Corporation was increased to 50 per cent, worker-members are not permitted to vote on conflict-of-interest issues such as pay scales and job classifications. Workers are paid a commission rather than the minimum wage.

In addition to dissolving the co-operative structure, the Ministry required that Able Courier change the project's emphasis from a business to a therapeutic setting. The job descriptions of the business managers have been rewritten and advertised as Program Co-ordinator and Case Manager, implying that mental-health professionals experienced in counselling and crisis intervention are required. Policies conforming to a therapeutic setting rather than to a business have been implemented.

Analysis of the Transformation

The failure of Able Courier to develop as a full-fledged worker co-operative does not indicate that the model cannot be applied to a psychiatric population. The ability of the workers to perform their jobs effectively was confirmed by the mental-health professionals involved. There were no reports of lost or damaged parcels and the manager was able to produce several letters of recommendation from satisfied customers. Clients noted the organized and professional manner in which the dispatchers and couriers conducted their business. Many of the mental-health professionals believed that the workers at Able Courier had a greater sense of responsibility towards the material entrusted to them than most couriers in regular businesses.

Critics expressed concern that the workers' slow pace and part-time schedules would make the project unworkable. While these observations cast doubt upon the viability of a worker co-operative composed of psychiatrically-disabled adults, such an analysis was premature and too simplistic. Several factors contributed to the workers' pace.

Many of Able Courier's workers had been unemployed for lengthy periods, and others had never held a job. These people, unaccustomed to positions of responsibility, were thrust into the roles of couriers and dispatchers. Many admitted they had been "nervous" their first few days on the job, but in retrospect, their fears had been unfounded. Most were able to perform the required tasks easily. The manager confirmed that the couriers' speed increased substantially with additional experience. He noted that some workers would always be slower than others due to illness-related factors, but speed was not an overwhelming obstacle to the project's success. The workers developed sufficient competence to allow the manager time away from the office. Both the couriers and the dispatchers expressed a desire to see the company expand its clientele and felt competent to deal with the increased workload.

Comparisons of Able Courier, in its growing phase, with established firms have led to damaging and inaccurate assessments of the workers' capabilities. The minimal emphasis that the Community Development Corporation Board placed on soliciting new clientele hampered the business' efficiency and profitability.

Able's workers confronted external barriers as they attempted to establish themselves as productive members of a worker co-operative. Most of the workers receive some form of social assistance. Individuals receiving this type of allowance are limited in the amount of additional income that they can earn without being penalized. Individuals earning over a prescribed amount (currently $150) have additional earnings deducted dollar-for-dollar from their assistance. This procedure served as a disincentive to Able Courier's workers to increase the number of hours worked and thus the amount of income earned.

If Able's workers achieved earnings in excess of the social-assistance limit, they also risked their eligibility for supported housing, publicly-funded mental health programs, and benefits that cover expensive daily medications. Without these medications, many would be hospitalized again.

While, the manager expressed confidence that the workers were able to perform their jobs efficiently, he noted that the environment at Able Courier was different from other courier companies. He was aware that the workers had special needs and encouraged them to discuss their problems with him. Some workers had experienced illness-related problems. However, Able's workers learned to monitor their ability to function, recognize a problem, and take appropriate action. There had not been a single incident in which workers put the business or clients' materials at risk. Workers who became ill, frequently returned to the job once they were feeling better.

The manager noted that medication side-effects and illness-related absences were not a problem for the business. If workers were unable to take their assigned shifts, they assumed responsibility for finding replacements. The worker would then notify the office of the change.

Advantages of a Worker Co-operative Model

Many of the Able workers had been labeled "permanently unemployable" by mental-health professionals. As a result, these individuals had little hope of achieving employment through the regular vocational-rehabilitation process. The worker co-operative provided an avenue through which people with little capital could participate in a business in which they shared ownership and control. Able workers could develop an environment that suited their needs. Members were able to establish flexible work schedules, tolerance for medically-related absences, and supportive-management strategies that would not have been available in most conventional enterprises. In addition, the worker co-operative guaranteed employment to individuals who faced the possibility of a recurrence in their illness. For many, previous bouts of illness had resulted in job-loss. Those who left Able for medical reasons were guaranteed a job upon recovery. Able's members benefited from the opportunity of working in a setting where co-workers understood their problems and offered support.

Participants reported that the business provided the opportunity to engage in meaningful and productive work, to increase social interaction, to develop one's self-esteem, to create a work history, to impose structure on their time, and to develop skills that would assist in subsequent employment. One worker stated:

> The job has given me a lot of confidence really, especially when I work a full day. I work two half-days and three full-days a week. When I work a full day I get a pretty good feeling of accomplishment because I guess that's what the rest of the world is doing. Most people work eight hours a day and I feel like I could go on to something else. I think I have a lot less problems and stress than I did before I took this job.

All individuals interviewed stated that their experience at Able Courier had generated a feeling of competence through having a "real" job and a more "normal" lifestyle. Some felt more comfortable with family and friends in that they were no longer perceived as "needing handouts." Workers also felt that their involvement in Able permitted them to contribute to the lives of other people either in their families or on the job. One participant summarized this sentiment:

> We have a very good comaraderie. . . .Everybody is in pretty good spirits most of the time. Every so often there's a disagreement or something but mostly we have a good comaraderie.

> There isn't really a hierarchy between the dispatchers and the couriers. It's more like the couriers rely on us and we rely on them, too. There's a lot of co-operation. I think we all respect each other. We're here to get the job done as best as possible.

The Able Courier experiment did not run its full course. The abrupt transformation of the business into a quasi-therapeutic setting limits the conclusions that can be drawn regarding the worker co-operative. However, the evidence suggests that a worker co-operative can provide a viable form of employment for some psychiatrically-disabled adults. There is no evidence that the workers were unable to perform the tasks required. Given the enthusiasm and commitment of the participants and progress already achieved by the workers, the Ministerial directive requiring dismantling of the co-operative appeared, at first glance, quite surprising.

Closer investigation revealed that the directive reflected biases that exist with the Ministry of Health regarding the potential of psychiatrically-disabled individuals. The Ministry's narrow definition of programs eligible for support reveals the contradiction between its rhetoric and practice. The Ministry claims its programs are designed to foster client independence. However, the Ministry supports expensive traditional workshop programs that fail to lead clients to permanent employment, while simultaneously refusing to support a project that put previously-labeled "unemployables" to work in a legitimate business thereby increasing their self-esteem and independence.

Financial problems arose from a decision to purchase rather than rent equipment. When forecast revenue could not be met, due to Able Courier's meager clientele, the business began to experience cash-flow difficulties. Had the capital expenditure been postponed and had increasing the clientele been a priority, the financial crisis and its consequences may well have been avoided. However, there was a majority of mental-health professionals on the newly restructured Board. These members were unfamiliar with business practices and conducive to accepting Ministry directives. When the Ministry requested restructuring the project and transforming the business into a therapeutic setting, the Board complied. Given their social-service background, Board members were able to identify with the project's new form. Moreover, most rationalized their compliance with the Ministry by suggesting that there was no alternative and that the changes would not affect the workers.

Policies that were indicative of a treatment program rather than a business were subsequently implemented. Able's workers were angered by new restrictions on their behavior. Many felt as though they were no longer trusted and were being stereotyped as incompetent and irresponsible. The message delivered by these directives asserts that the Ministry feels that the psychiatrically-disabled are incapable of performing responsible and productive work. The real concern of the Ministry seems to be the provision of low-cost therapeutic treatment. The restructured Able Courier was hailed as an example of a successful day-treatment program as it required minimal front-line staff to "look after" a large client population. The Ministry failed to recognize the therapeutic value of work. Moreover, the change in Able's structure to a quasi-therapeutic setting will in all probability reinforce feelings of inferiority so prevalent in the disabled.

The progress achieved by Able's workers in a short time was ignored. The Ministry was unwilling to entertain the idea that disabled individuals with some support could operate a business independent of its supervision even though similar projects have been operating successfully in Poland and Hungary for 40 years and are on the increase elsewhere in North America.[10]

The programs offered by many sheltered workshops do not constitute rehabilitation in the sense of providing clients with the opportunity to develop job skills that will improve their participation in the labour force. Rather in sheltered workshops the provision of low-cost labour under the guise of rehabilitation creates an underclass that performs work for various industries at minimal cost. Meanwhile, taxpayers pick up the tab for this labour in the form of public subsidies to the workshops.

A test case presently before the Courts may change this situation. The plaintiff argues that traditional workshop programs contravene the rights of the disabled as set out in the Canadian Charter of Human Rights. If the court rules against workshop programs, the disabled will no longer be required to work for meager wages in day-treatment programs. As a consequence of the loss of revenue generated by client labour, the cost of these day-treatment programs will skyrocket. It is likely that this situation will result in a radical re-evaluation of rehabilitation and employment opportunities for disabled individuals. As businesses and government have been reluctant to employ people with special needs, the worker co-operative model may be adopted as an alternative to high-cost day-treatment programs.

A Development Strategy

Co-operatives have traditionally been developed to provide security to those who are disadvantaged. The worker co-operative offers the disabled stable employment and democratic control over the workplace. The model allows handicapped individuals to develop support systems within the business. Management that is sensitive to the special needs of the disabled, flexible work schedules, and tolerance for medically-related absences give individuals who have been excluded from the conventional labour force the opportunity to develop skills and assume greater independence over a period of time.

Some handicapped individuals placed in regular businesses have experienced discrimination and isolation. The co-operative model allows the disabled to determine the extent to which they work alongside non-handicapped individuals. For example, in Poland, co-operatives that began with an exclusively handicapped membership are now allowing up to 30 per cent of their members to be non-handicapped. This policy normalizes the work environment without eclipsing the accomplishments of the disabled founders.

In Canada, despite the barriers that are currently imposed by bureaucratic restrictions and lack of interest among financial investors, several worker co-operative projects have been created. The activities of these enterprises range from producing hand-painted clothing, domestic furniture, and decorative items to delivery and maintenance services. Churchill Park Greenhouse Co-op in Moose Jaw provides the disadvantaged with employment in vegetable production.[11]

Government policies will have to change in order for a worker co-operative development strategy to proceed. Logically, the Ministry of Health could provide the impetus to developing worker co-operatives as an alternative to treatment programs that maintain client dependence. Given the Ministry's current responsibility for funding treatment and rehabilitation programs for the disabled, it seems reasonable that the Ministry would prefer to channel its resources into programs that facilitate client independence. However, the Ministry is characterized by inflexible policies that reflect a narrow perspective on health and well-being. The Ministry currently defines its mandate in terms of treatment programs for sick individuals. Overlooking the therapeutic value of work, the Ministry seems to feel that if one is well enough to work, one does not need its assistance. A fundamental change in policy and perspective would be required for the Ministry of Health to become the driving force behind the development of worker co-operatives for the disabled.

Alternatives to current policies for the disabled are being developed in several of Canada's urban centres. Recognition that large numbers of disadvantaged people are unemployed or underemployed has motivated other provincial ministries and several municipalities to create community economic development initiatives. For example, a City of Toronto Community Economic Development Committee has recommended that the City establish a Technical Resource Centre and co-ordinate a Financial Assistance Corporation to facilitate the development of economic enterprises that provide employment to those who have been bypassed by the conventional labour market. This recommendation recognizes that while the long-term goal of these enterprises is to attain financial self-sufficiency, some ventures may require an extended period of nurturing. A community economic development program that provides technical and financial assistance reduces many of the obstacles confronted by handicapped entrepreneurs.

Full-scale development of the model would have to be facilitated by policy revisions across various levels of government. These revisions would include changing income restrictions so that workers in transition from their dependent status would not be penalized for increasing the number of hours worked. Subsidized housing and medical benefits should not be linked to social-assistance payments and treatment programs. Social assistance should be made immediately available to workers whose disability prevents them from continuing to participate in the business. The Ministry of Health should relax restrictions on programs eligible for funding. Limiting support to therapeutic treatment programs perpetuates the role of clients as passive recipients of services.

A developmental model in which decision-making is initially shared between the members of a worker co-operative and the Board of a Community Development Corporation provides the disabled with the opportunity to acquire the skills and experience to become self-sufficient. Members of the Community Development Corporation would offer assistance in business planning and financing, and ensure the accountability of management. Worker representation on the Board and on various committees would facilitate education and experience. Exclusive control of decision-making would be transferred to the co-operative as the workers acquired appropriate skills. The period during which the Community Development Corporation would function in this nurturing role would depend upon the characteristics and capacities of the workers in each enterprise.

The worker co-operative provides an alternative to the high-cost day-treatment programs currently offered by the Ministry. The worker co-operative model acknowledges that the disabled have special needs in developing and controlling their workplace. As the abilities of the handicapped are increasingly recognized in North America, the worker co-operative model provides an avenue through which the disabled can develop their potential and achieve a greater level of independence.

146

Notes

[1]L. Conte, "Manpower Policy and the Disabled Person: An International Perspective," *Rehabilitation Literature*, 43, No. 5 (1982), 132-133.

[2]Conte,"Manpower Policy and the Disabled Person," p. 133.

[3]Conte, "Manpower Policy and the Disabled Person," p. 133.

[4]S. Olshansky, "Changing Vocational Behavior through Normalization," in *Normalization*, ed. W. Wolfensberger (Toronto: National Institute on Mental Retardation, 1972), pp. 150-163.

[5]E. J. Thomas, "Problems of Disability from the Perspective of Role Theory," *Journal of Health and Human Behavior*, 7 (1966).

[6]E. Markowe, "Psychiatric Disability and Unemployment," *British Journal of Social Medicine*, 9 (1955), 39-46; W. Richardson, "An Experiment in Resettling the Disabled," *Rehabilitation*, 17, No. 2 (1956); and I. Bronks, "A Follow-Up Survey of Psychiatric Patients Referred to Industrial Rehabilitation Units," *Rehabilitation*, 1098, No. 65, 5-10.

[7]W. Anthony, G. Buell, S. Sharratt, and M. Althoss, "The Efficacy of Psychiatric Rehabilitation," *Psychological Bulletin*, 78 (1972) 447-456; W. Anthony, M. Cohen, and R. Vitalo, "The Measurement of Rehabilitation Outcome," *Schizophrenia Bulletin*, 4 (1984), 365-383; W. Anthony, J. Howell, and K. Danley, *The Vocational Rehabilitation of the Psychiatrically-Disabled* (Jamaica, New York: The Chronically Mentally Ill Research and Services, 1984); W. Anthony and G. Dion, *Psychiatric Rehabilitation: A Rehabilitation Research Review* (Washington, D.C.: National Rehabilitation Information Center, 1986); and D. Wasylenki, P. Goering, W. Lancee, L. Fischer and S. Freeman, "Psychiatric Aftercare in a Metropolitan Setting," *Canadian Journal of Psychiatry*, 30 (1985), 329-366.

[8]W. Anthony and A. Blanch, "Supported Employment for Persons who are Psychiatrically Disabled: An Historical and Conceptual Approach," *Psychosocial Rehabilitation Journal*, 11, No. 2 (1987), 5.

[9]P. Holmes, "Dialogue on Supported Employment: A Discussion Paper," Toronto: Ontario Ministry of Labour, 1987.

[10]Conte, *Manpower Policy and the Disabled Person*, pp. 132-133.

[11]Skip McCarthy, "Churchill Park Greenhouse Co-op: A Community Service Co-op Conversion," *Worker Co-op*, 5, No. 3 (1985), 22-23.

Chapter 7

Co-operatives: Ethical Foundations

Gregory Baum

From the beginning the co-operative movement was a self-help enterprise. Men and women, unable to find work and make a living under the existing economic conditions, organized their economic activity on the basis of solidarity and co-operation. What was operative was people's material self-interest. At the same time, the co-operative movement produced an ethical critique of the social conditions created by capitalism and presented itself as a social enterprise that, if widely accepted, could create an alternative order of society, a co-operative commonwealth. The material self-interest motivating the movement was accompanied by other more universal values. Co-operatism had an ethical foundation.

The Ethical Critique

The Rochdale Principles of 1848 imply an entire set of social values. 'Open membership' rejected the barriers created by religious, ethnic, and gender discrimination pervasive in the social order. 'One-member/one-vote' affirmed human equality against the cultural heritage derived from the age of privilege. 'Democratic control' expressed the Enlightenment ideal that people were destined to be 'subjects' or responsible agents of the institutions to which they belonged, and 'co-operative ownership'

147

affirmed solidarity and co-operation against the individualism and competitiveness characteristic of capitalist society. 'Limited return on capital' signified the repudiation of the greed implicit in capitalist maximization of profit, and 'distribution of surplus to the members' offered an alternative to exploitation and the overcoming of wage labour. Finally, 'education of the members' was intended to make co-operatives a source of social criticism in society.

This remarkable ethical critique of the emerging liberal society embodied values derived from traditional and radical sources. The Tory critique of liberal society lamented the loss of community, the emergence of individualism, the waning of solidarity, and the victory of greed. The Radicals (socialists and anarchists) shared with liberals the Enlightenment hope that the social world could be reconstructed along rational lines. Radicals also anticipated progress. Yet, with the Tories, they lamented liberal individualism and the breakdown of solidarity. Radicals differed from the Tories in their almost religious yearning for social equality: They were egalitarians. They repudiated the conservative vision of an organic society with its connatural hierarchy, and they opposed the domination of the new ruling class, the bourgeoisie, created by liberal society. The Radicals re-interpreted the liberal idea that humans were meant to be the 'subjects' of their lives by giving it a social or collective meaning. By their rational nature people were destined to become jointly responsible for their collective existence.

Co-operatism had an original vision that combined values derived from different sources. Like conservatives, supporters of co-operatism treasured social solidarity, community, and co-operation; and like the radicals, they opposed hierarchy, promoted egalitarianism, and called for co-responsibility. Like conservatives, they feared centralization (as did the anarchists) and shied away from class struggle as a strategy that undermined social solidarity. Yet like liberals and radicals, they endorsed the Enlightenment principle that people were responsible for their history and hence that human progress was possible.

Engaging in ethical-philosophical reflections in his early writings, Karl Marx arrived at social positions that had an extraordinary affinity with co-operatism.[1] The young Marx asked whether people were by nature selfish or whether selfishness was a character trait produced by an economic system based on competition. He adopted the latter position. Because the social relations of work largely create human consciousness and character, the domination of the market produces people preoccupied with promoting themselves at the expense of others. It is quite useless, Marx argued, to give people sermons inviting them to cultivate the love of neighbour. The structures in which people live have a more powerful impact on consciousness than ethical ideals. What will enable people to leave behind the selfishness into which they have been socialized is the creation of jointly-owned economic enterprises that demand daily co-operation and participation. Here people's material self-interest summons them to collaboration and solidarity. Here people will become selfless and realize their true humanity. The human, Marx argued, is a 'Gattungswesen,' a being that realizes itself in identification with the entire species.

In his early writings, Marx also introduced a concept of alienation that was based on ethical-philosophical not on purely economic considerations. People suffer alienation from their humanity whenever they are prevented from assuming responsibility for the institutions to which they belong, be these institutions economic, social, or political. Workers are to be co-owners. Society is to be participatory. People are meant to be the makers of their destiny, the 'subjects' of their world.

These ethical ideals are close to co-operatism. Yet they did not survive in Marx's later, more scientific work when he defined alienation more narrowly in terms of the separation of workers from the ownership of the goods produced by them. Nor did the later Marx engage in ethical reflections on the overcoming of human selfishness. Marx, the economist, and many of his followers were embarrassed by the metaphysical implications of his early writings. Was there a human nature? And if so, was an ethical imperative built into this human nature?

By contrast, the co-operative movement was connected to its ethical foundation. It did not claim to offer a 'scientific' remedy to society's problems. The important founding personalities, whether they were secular or religious, were men and women with strong moral convictions. They were critical of capitalism and capitalistic values. Their main interest was not theoretical but practical. They organized the movement and focused their attention on the practical problems of co-operatives. It is my impression that they did not feel the need to engage in a theoretical clarification of the movement's ethical foundation.

One of the reasons for this relative silence was the fact that the members of the movement differed among themselves. What held them together were the principles of co-operatism. Some members were secular, while others were religious, and as we shall see, the religious co-operators believed there was a special affinity between co-operatism and Christian ethics. But the religious members did not want to make religion the big issue. The big issue was co-operation between members.

The co-operators also had different political views. Some members looked upon co-operatism as a radical movement destined to transform capitalist society into a co-operative commonwealth. Others did not despair of liberal society: They thought that the creation of a significant co-operative sector would produce a qualitative transformation of the economy -- part privately-owned, part publicly-owned, and part co-operatively-owned. Other members regarded the co-operative movement as useful and important for the participants but did not think it had a mission for society as a whole. Because the primary need was to stick together and work in co-operation, co-operators preferred to go easy on theory and adopt a pragmatic approach.

It may be relevant to note in this context that in modern society ethical discourse has disappeared from all levels of public life. We have learned to rely increasingly on the sciences, including the social sciences, conceived of as objective, value-free ways of knowing. With Kant we like to distinguish between facts and values. What counts for the scientific knowledge of reality are the facts. Facts are hard. Values are soft. Scientists, engineers, and administrators must learn to bracket value considerations and rely on the scientific approach. What has happened in our society is that all social issues, whether unemployment or the deterioration of the soil, are looked upon as technical problems. Yet most people -- in my opinion -- are well aware in their heart of hearts that social problems are ultimately moral issues.

In a technological society moral discourse often appears old-fashioned. Scientific positivism creates the intellectual mood for liberalism and more radical thought. Thus the left-wing critics of the present order also hesitate to speak about values. The word 'ethics' sounds moralistic to them. It suggests the preaching of private morality without sensitivity to the social evil produced by the contradictions of society. Some radicals look upon ethics as an ideology of the dominant classes demanding that people be polite, submissive, and patient. Yet at this time, the growing inhumanity of the age and the present crises of capitalism and socialism impel more and more social thinkers to pay attention to values and engage in ethical reflection.

Religion and Co-operatism

While co-operatism as a whole was not preoccupied with theoretical questions, the religious people involved in it paid a great deal of attention to its ethical foundation. They believed that co-operatism had a special affinity with Christian values. In England, a group that called its philosophy Christian Socialism supported the co-operative movement; on the European continent, Christians in the Protestant and the Catholic traditions involved themselves in the co-operative movement on the basis of specifically Christian convictions.[2] They argued that the biblical vision of life favoured co-operation over competition. They denounced the emerging industrial capitalism as unjust, exploitative, and inhuman. They appealed to the divine vocation of human beings to build a just and fraternal (sororal) world. They were not afraid to endorse the modern concept of co-responsibility because they recognized it to be grounded in very ancient human aspirations, including the social ideals contained in biblical history. God's covenant made with Israel after the rescue from political and economic oppression was based on the co-responsibility of all its members, male and female. Even the maids and servants employed to do the laundry had to give their free consent before the covenant was validated.

These Christians, minorities in their churches, supported co-operatism because they saw it as a revolutionary strategy for the reconstruction of society. They appreciated its conservative respect for social solidarity and traditional values. These Christians were often suspicious of socialism in the strict sense. They were uncomfortable with an overall plan to transfer the ownership of the means of production to society; they feared both the power necessary to implement such a transfer and the centralization of responsibility that could result from it. They were also unhappy about the militant secularism adopted by the socialists, especially on the European continent.

The co-operative movement in Canada, especially in Québec, the West, and Nova Scotia, was strongly supported by church people. In Québec people felt that co-operatism had a special affinity with 'subsidiarity,' a principle of Catholic social ethics. The principle of subsidiarity affirms that if a small community or organization is capable of attending to its needs, then higher authority has no moral right to interfere in its life. This is a principle that stands against unjustified centralization. (Curiously enough, the Catholic Church hesitates to apply this principle in its own organization.) Subsidiarity is a traditional formulation of 'small is beautiful.'

In Western Canada it was the Protestant Social Gospel that produced widespread support for the co-operative movement. This Gospel was based upon a democratic, self-determining, anti-hierarchical tradition of British Protestantism that created the spiritual link to co-operatism. In Free Church Protestantism, co-responsibility has always been an essential religious principle. Moreover, the special historical conditions under which the western farmers had to make their living pushed them to adopt a wider analysis of the exploitative structures of the Canadian economy. As a consequence many of them became socialists, religiously-motivated socialists. This joining of co-operative and socialist activity in the prairie provinces was perhaps the most important historical development responsible for the creation of the Co-operative Commonwealth Federation (CCF). The Regina

Manifesto of 1933 that committed the new party to an original, Canadian form of socialism included a paragraph pledging support for the co-operative movement. From the beginning Canadian socialism tried to integrate co-operatism as a decentralizing principle.

The Antigonish Movement in Nova Scotia, founded in the late twenties, was of Catholic inspiration. Because the movement was regarded as radical and controversial in the culturally-conservative world of those days, Father Moses Coady, one of its founders, was obliged to produce a theological defense of co-operative principles. We owe to him a literature that reveals vigour and originality.[3] Because the open membership and the implicit ecumenism of the movement offended many Catholics, Coady presented a reasoned yet passionate plea for economic co-operation among people of different religious convictions. He was disgusted by religious prejudice. Coady tried to show that the co-operative philosophy of the Antigonish Movement was in keeping with the papal social teaching of that time. Co-operatism, he argued, was as critical of liberal and socialist economics as were the Popes. For tactical purposes he exaggerated the affinity between co-operatism and papal social teaching. In fact, at that time Pope Pius XI proposed economic corporatism as the solution for the crisis created by the Depression and only made the slightest hint in favour of the right of workers to 'co-determination.' Co-ownership was not even envisaged in Pius' papal teaching.

Religious members of the co-operative movement showed more theoretical interest in its moral foundation than did the secular participants. The values of the co-operative movement were also attractive to people of religious traditions other than Christianity. Jews, secular and religious, have supported the principles of co-operatism. So have Hindus and members of other Asian religions.

Recent Trends in the Church

More recently, the social theoreticians of the Christian churches have elaborated an ethical critique of capitalism and, in this context, provide new and stronger arguments in support of worker co-operatives. This shift to the left on the part of the major churches is due to two historical circumstances: first, in the sixties, the emergence of Third World liberation movements and second, more recently, the Western turn to neo-conservatism.

The liberation movements in the Third World affected the churches' policy. Typical here is the experience of the Geneva-based World Council of Churches (WCC) founded in 1948.[4] At first it represented the theology and social ethics of churches in the North Atlantic nations and considered itself the teacher of the churches in the colonies and former colonies. When at the 'Church and Society' meeting organized in Geneva in 1966, the majority of participants represented Third World countries, a theological explosion took place that eventually changed the entire orientation of the World Council. The Fourth WCC Assembly at Uppsala in 1968 recommended the creation of the Commission on the Churches' Participation in Development (CCPD), which was to concentrate ecumenical theological thinking on economic questions. The Commission, founded in 1970, became active in its critical research and inventive in its ethical proposals. Its detailed reports eventually persuaded the members of the Council to redefine its orientation as the option for the poor and oppressed. The CCPD generated an ethical critique of global capitalism: It denounced the exploitation of workers, especially in the Third World; the monopoly of power exercised by trans-national corporations to the detriment of the common good, especially in the Third World; and the destructive ecological impact of uncontrolled industrial development, again especially in the Third World. It formulated the new ecumenical social ethics as the quest for a 'just, participatory, and sustainable' society. 'Just' refers to the overcoming of exploitation, 'participatory' to the overcoming of domination, and 'sustainable' to the overcoming of ecological destruction.

The WWC supports people-owned and people-managed

economic institutions. The remaking of the global economy must break the stranglehold of the trans-nationals and create socially-owned industries; at the same time it must avoid the concentration of power in the hands of the state. Societies must make use of their governments to steer the economy in accordance with their own needs and global requirements, but they must also ensure that capital is decentralized through community-based and worker-based economic institutions. Worker co-operatives appear as part of a strategy for global economic reconstruction.

The shift of orientation at the WCC is paradigmatic for what has happened in other international ecclesiastical bodies, for example, the Roman Catholic Church, the Anglican Communion, and the more recently-founded international federations of Reformed and Lutheran and other Protestant Churches. I might add that the social position adopted by the United Church of Canada reflects the approach of the WCC.

The WCC and many of the Protestant bodies tend to defend their radical social ethics with biblical teaching. The Third World churches see more clearly that the biblical God demands a just society, that God evaluates a society in accordance with the way it treats its weakest members, that God repudiates Pharaonic rule and all structures of domination, and that God summons people to tame nature or transform it into a garden and, in doing so, to become responsible stewards of creation. God has condemned as idolotry the limitless attachment to wealth, power, and prestige.

Worker Ownership in Catholic Theology

Roman Catholic social ethics also invoke the biblical heritage, yet the social ethics are expressed in the language of rational principles derived from dialogue with social philosophy and political science. The recent shift to the left in Catholic teaching has assigned a central place to two richly-defined ethical principles, 'the preferential option for the poor' and 'the priority of labour over capital.'[5] In this context worker ownership of industries receives special attention.

To understand the evolution of Catholic social teaching we must pay attention to the impact of the Third World churches and, more recently, to the turn to neo-conservatism that has taken place in the North Atlantic nations. Neo-conservatism refers to a set of economic policies and the promotion of related cultural values. In the opinion of Pope John Paul II and the Canadian Catholic bishops, world capitalism has entered a crisis. Unless the present movement can be stopped, we are moving into a more brutal and repressive phase of capitalism. The Canadian bishops, in particular, argue that the unwritten contract between capital and society, worked out after World War II, is coming apart at the seams. This unwritten contract, based on Keynesian economics, guaranteed full employment, welfare provisions, and respect for labour organizations. In our day the ideal of full employment has been abandoned, welfare legislation is being dismantled, and war is waged against labour unions. What is taking place at this time, according to the Canadian bishops, is the re-organization of capital within trans-national corporations. The free-enterprise ideology of the self-regulating market is used to legitimate the removal of regulations, to destroy the social structures of solidarity, and to make honourable an indifference to the common good. What has taken place, according to the Canadian bishops, is the widening of the gap between rich and poor and rich and poor countries and the concentration of economic power in the hands of an ever-shrinking elite.

The new economic policies are accompanied by a discourse promoting new values. We live in a tough world. Each person must learn to take care of him or herself. What happens is the fittest survive. There are no more free lunches. In the past, society lived beyond its means: We were too generous, we took care of people, we made them passive. This has resulted in an enormous national debt. The first duty of government is to cut spending. Our workers were pampered. We have allowed the unions to become too powerful and push up the workers' wages. It is their fault that we cannot compete on the world market. We have to learn to tighten our belts. We must learn that the well-being of all depends on the economic success of capitalist enterprises. These entrepreneurs, the wealth creators, deserve tax breaks and subsidies; they merit their riches and the high style in which they live. Egalitarianism is simply a form of envy, a lack of love and respect. And so it goes on. An economic system based on self-promotion is blessed by a set of values that make selfishness appear appropriate. In the old-fashioned language of the church, sinful social structures are being justified by a set of false values.

The leaders of the mainline churches in Canada and the U.S.A. have resisted the neo-conservative trend, even if the majority of church members seem to have accepted it. The policy statements of all the churches defend social solidarity and joint responsibility for the well-being of all. This is the context in which the Canadian Catholic bishops have worked out their radical social ethics.

This radical social-ethics statement is similar to the position adopted by the WCC. Both share the same perspective, the option for the poor, the decision to look at society from the viewpoint of its victims. The Canadian Catholic bishops argue in a somewhat more technical way that the human ills produced by the present economic system can be overcome only through a significant reconstruction of the economy. The principle, 'the priority of labour over capital,' means among other things that the economy must be rebuilt around the needs of labour (i.e., the needs of the population) not around the ambitions of capital. Doing that requires a twofold move. The economy needs responsible, democratically-controlled planning for natural resources and for necessities such as food and housing. At the same time, this centralizing trend needs balancing by a decentralizing trend, more specifically by the decentralization of capital, the break-up of the giant corporations, and the promotion of alternative models of economic development such as worker-owned and community-owned industries. The tension between the centralizing and the decentralizing will protect personal freedom in society.

158

A Third Way

The bishops lament that many Canadians think that the only choice before them is between capitalism and communism. Society is threatened when power is concentrated in the state or in the giant economic corporations. At one time Catholic social teaching feared above all the excessive power of the state, while more recently the warnings are often directed against the excessive power of the trans-nationals. On his visit to Canada in 1984 Pope John Paul II condemned economic imperialism, especially in the context of North-South interdependence.[6] Planning must go hand in hand with new forms of social ownership, including worker co-operatives. As in the documents of the WCC, the call for worker co-ops is part of a wider strategy for the reconstruction of the global economy.

This emphasis on worker co-ops finds special confirmation in the ethical reflections entertained by Pope John Paul II in his 1981 encyclical on labour.[7] Here, he argues that the ethical principle, 'the priority of labour,' means that capital must be in the service of labour and not the other way around. But what precisely does 'serving labour' involve? It requires that management must use society's wealth to renew technologies and to serve the well-being of all those who labour. Because industries have become so interconnected and dependent on the institutions of society, the whole of society must be regarded as labouring; the profit made by the industries must not only serve the workers but also society in its entirety.

More than that, 'capital serving labour' also means that management must not regard workers as part of capital as if workers were 'objects,' but that on the contrary management must respect workers as 'subjects,' as responsible agents. In the language adopted by John Paul II, an economic system is ethical only if workers are 'the subject' of production. We note in this connection that when the Pope uses the word 'worker,' he refers first of all to manual and clerical workers, yet he also includes persons working in management. He argues that the value and dignity of labour is such that workers are entitled to participate in the decisions regarding the use of their products and hence the surplus value and the organization of the work process. This is what being 'subject of production' means.

What are the conditions that favour the priority of labour over capital? The Polish Pope argues convincingly that the nationalization of industries is no guarantee that they will be managed in the service of labour. Public administrations may run the industries to enhance the power of the government or to maximize the profit on the world market. For John Paul II, in contrast with Marx, the big issue is not the 'ownership' but the 'use' of captial. There is no final institutional guarantee that capital will serve labour. The highest probability that this priority will be observed is given when the workers themselves become the owners of the giant workbench at which they labour. If they become the owners then there is greater likelihood that the industry will serve their well-being and that of society as a whole.

According to the ethical reflections of John Paul II, wage labour must ultimately be overcome. The present separation of work from ownership is unjust. Eventually workers must become the co-owners of industries, which means that they will work for themselves as they work in the service of society. In this context worker co-ops are not just part of a wider strategy for economic reconstruction, but they are also seen as an end in themselves, as the most human mode of organizing work, as an enterprise that allows men and women to work for themselves, to realize themselves through their work and at the same time to labour in the service of the wider community.

Notes

[1]Karl Marx, "On the Jewish Question" and "Contribution to the Critique of Hegel's Philosophy of Right," in *Karl Marx: Early Writings*, ed. and intro. T.B. Bottomore (New York: Ungar, 1964), pp. 3-59.

[2]"Co-operatives," *Encylopedia Britannica*, 6 (1967).

[3]Moses Coady, *Masters of their own Destiny* (New York: Harper & Row, 1939); and Alex Laidlaw, *The Man from Margaree: Writings and Speeches of M.M. Coady* (Toronto: McClelland & Stewart, 1971).

[4]For a brief survey, see Ulrich Duchrow, *Global Economy* (Geneva: WCC Publications, 1987), pp. 71-83.

[5]G. Baum and D. Cameron, *Ethics and Economics* (Toronto: Lorimer, 1964), pp. 40-51.

[6]G. Baum, "John Paul II's Social Teaching in Canada," *Theology and Society*, (1967) 88-103, 96.

[7]See G. Baum, *The Priority of Labor: A Commentary on LABOREM EXECERCENS* (New York: Paulist Press, 1982).

Chapter 8

Social History of
Worker Co-operatives in Québec

Alain Bridault and Ginette Lafrenière

The renaissance of worker co-operatives in Europe during the 1970s was echoed here in Canada, particularly in Québec. But, as was the case in Europe, the Québec phenomenon was not so much a renaissance, as the beginning of a new co-operative sector. Over the past century, there were a small number of worker co-operatives, isolated and ephemeral, but nevertheless of importance because they left a historical trail that influenced the growth of the 1970s. It is only in the mid-1970s that their development surpasses isolated examples and could thus qualify as a social phenomenon.[1] By 1985 worker co-operatives were able to create their own organization -- the Québec Federation of Worker co-operatives.[2]

We begin this chapter with the "pre-history" of Québec worker co-operatives, starting with the first "generation" of worker-production co-operatives in 1865. We will then turn to the forestry co-operatives of the 1930s, and lastly an exceptional but isolated case, Harpell, in 1945. Following that we shall analyze the Tricofil experience of the 1970s as it serves as a transition to the development of the current worker co-operative movement. In conclusion, the social basis of Québec's worker co-operatives will be analyzed.

The Pre-History

Research carried out on European worker co-operatives depicted a direct correlation between the existence of a specific legal framework and the development of the sector. Understandably, legislation is but one of many factors that favours the creation of worker co-operatives. Yet in Lower Canada (Québec prior to confederation) there did not exist any kind of legislation specifically for co-operatives, and furthermore anti-labour laws permitted little or no association. It would seem, however, that certain groups utilized the cover of mutual societies to experiment with "quasi" worker co-operatives, especially in times of strikes or unemployment.

An Ephemeral First Generation: Co-operatives Linked to the Labour Movement

In 1865 (in what would constitute the first Québec worker co-operative), "La coopérative de construction de Québec" provided work for approximately 40 men.[3] This co-operative was part of the "Société des charpentiers de navire," which itself was founded in 1861 and was comprised of about 750 members. At that time naval construction for the British Empire brought prosperity to Canada's eastern ports. A co-operative bakery was created by the "Grande Association," a worker organization founded in 1867 by Médéric Lanctot. With the influence of the American organization, The Knights of Labour, we can observe a concerted effort in Québec to develop worker-production co-operatives.

As in France and England, Québec unions and worker-production co-operatives were intimately linked in defending the concerns of workers. The worker co-operative permitted unionized workers to support themselves during long strikes. Historians have noted many examples of striking workers forming worker co-operatives: the first luggage co-operative in 1887, the Franklin Co-operative Press in 1888, a co-operative of shoemakers in 1887, the Point-Saint Charles industrial co-operative in 1886, and a cigar production co-operative in 1893. Other than the cigar co-operative which endured to the 1930s, these first worker co-operatives rapidly disappeared.

After the founding of the labour party in 1904 and after the election of the first labour parliamentarian, A.T. Lépine, and with the influence of European movements, the socialist-labour movement received a second wind. A "socialist commune" was established in Montréal in 1907. The socialist leader, Albert Saint-Martin, and a nucleus of militants created Québec's version of Rochdale. It included the esperanto co-operative (two co-operative stores), a collective farm (the Kanado) started in 1914, a newspaper "Spartakus," and a printing press which later became a co-operative in 1932. A labour university was also created but disallowed in 1933.

These first experimental worker co-operatives did not enjoy a future. Unlike France and Italy, Québec did not have the necessary support system for co-operatives. It is important to remember that up until the first world war French Canadian society was predominantly rural. The other co-operative movements which took hold at the time corresponded to the sociological needs of the people: credit unions (financial co-operatives) that provided credit and protection against usury and marketing and purchasing co-operatives for farmers. Therefore, worker co-operatives directed to the craftspersons and labourers of urban centres corresponded to the specific needs of only a small proletarized minority. It is important to note that the strong influence of the Catholic Church and its virulent anti-socialist campaigns did manage to contain any tendency towards the development of worker co-operatives during this period.

The Second Wave: Forestry Co-operatives

When the Antigonish movement started its study groups during the Great Depression, not only did it influence the creation of forestry and fishing co-operatives in Nova Scotia but also in the Acadian peninsula and amongst French Canadian communities on the other side of the Baie des Chaleurs in Gaspésie. The first forestry co-operative was founded in 1938 in Grande-Vallée. By 1970, 166 forestry co-operatives had been created in such places as in Gaspésie, Saguenay lac St-Jean, on the North coast, in Abitibi Témiscamingue, and in the

Appalachians.[4] Forestry co-operatives were created primarily in rural areas where public forests constituted close to 90 per cent of woodland. Most survived only a few years; others, however, are more than 30 years old today with multi-million dollar sales.[5] The workforce for these forestry co-operatives consisted of subsistence farmers who wanted to supplement their meager earnings. At that time, outside the rich agricultural lands of the Saint-Laurence basin, farming was subsistence only -- a few cows and animals, and a large garden. Other than some revenues from the sale of cream to small co-operative creameries which survived up until the 1960s, an essential part of the "habitants'" income came from the labour of father and sons in the large timber yards during winter. The paper mills, which exploited the large concessions granted by the government for public forests, contracted the timber-cutting to "jobbers" who in turn hired the lumberjacks. They lived in unhealthy quarters and worked for pitiful wages based upon the cords of wood that they cut. Even today, the Irving timberyards in New Brunswick continue this type of exploitation.

The forestry co-operatives were created to fight against exploitation. Often encouraged by the parish priest, they entered successfully into competition with the jobbers. However, the original forestry co-operatives differed from other forms of worker co-operatives in several ways. Some forestry co-operatives were similar to agricultural co-operatives, that is, semi-autonomous owners co-operating in the marketing of wood and in the purchase of machinery. Others did not even own basic machinery. They could be described as manpower co-operatives (a term used by the International Bureau of Labour), similar to the Italian "Bracchianti" agricultural co-operatives.[6]

The modern forestry co-operatives in Québec differ from their forerunners because they are mature businesses with a strong membership base and with considerable assets in equipment, factories, etc. Yet they, too, remain apart from the other worker co-operatives of the province. The 32 forestry co-operatives and their 3300 members have formed their own organization, a council, rather than joining the provincial federation.

The Post-War: An Exceptional Case, Harpell[7]

In 1945, James-John Harpell, philanthropist and proprietor of two printing presses in Toronto and Saint-Anne de Bellevue, decided at the time of his retirement to bring the businesses under the control of his workers by converting them into worker co-operatives -- The Garden City Press Co-operative in Toronto and Harpell's Co-operative in Québec (the latter being changed to the French name, "L'imprimerie coopérative Harpell," in 1977). James J. Harpell's vision extended far beyond the creation of a worker co-operative. Like Robert Owen of New Lanark, Harpell also created a model community in Ste-Anne de Bellevue in 1919 for the press workers. Developed as a "garden city" in the image of its European and American counterparts, this community was part of Harpell's heritage to his workers. In 1922, Harpell also founded the Institute of Industrial Arts for professional and continuing education of the workers.

The Harpell Co-operative Press was exceptional because it was created from the conversion of a healthy business. It was for a long time the largest Canadian worker co-operative both in terms of revenues and its working members. In 1986 it had nearly 200 workers and about $12 million of sales.

1970: The Emergence of a Small Diversified Sector

The First "Wave" and its Failures

In 1975 the first research dedicated exclusively to worker co-operatives was undertaken in Québec.[8] The anonymous authors at the "Co-operative Center of Social Political Research" used three categories: self-managed co-operatives, co-operatives for the unemployed, and co-operatives for local economic development.

The first two types, involving the unemployed without any professional qualifications, survived with great difficulty. They were financed by job-creation programs which appeared at the beginning of the 1970s. Their lack of capital limited these co-ops to small-crafts production. Given the cost of their products, they had a bourgeois clientele. However, the members lacked professional qualifications and their products were lacking in quality. As such these co-operatives were not viable financially and most disappeared shortly after receiving their grants. Those which did survive involved workers with a professional education and a specific craft, for example, the "Parminou Theatre Cooperative." Taxi and blueberry co-operatives also evolved at this time.[9]

A Second Exceptional Case: Tricofil

In 1973, when the Regent Knitting textile factory of St-Jérôme closed its doors, the workers decided to buy the factory in order to save their jobs. Similar to the LIP in France and the Meridian Motorcycle in England, Tricofil became, because of intense publicity, a cause célèbre. Tricofil was, at the beginning of the 1970s, seen as the finest example of a self-managed firm. This experience revived the worker co-operative movement in Québec and the role of organized labour in worker co-operatives. Even though Tricofil did not become incorporated as a worker co-operative till the very end of its existence in 1981, its ultimate failure as a business was a setback to the movement. The disenchantment following Tricofil was due in part to expectations that were raised.[10]

Québec Labour Co-operatives in the 1980s

Due to the Québec government's actions in establishing both a special aid program and a specific legislative framework, worker co-operative development took off during the 1980s. By 1985, 178 worker co-operatives with 7,341 members were registered.[11] They furnished around five per cent of the total of small-business manufacturers and roughly 0.4 per cent of the total of Québec workers. Other noteworthy characteristics are as follows:

1. Of 178 co-operatives, 104 were founded between 1981 and 1986, 33 between 1975 and 1986, and 41 between 1940 and 1976.

2. The co-operatives are predominantly in the primary sector (natural resources) and the service sector (see Table 8.1).

3. Worker co-operatives are found predominantly in the peripheral regions of the province. The large region of Montréal has only 23 co-operatives, 22 per cent the total. Similar numbers are found in Saguenay and in Abitibi.

4. With the exception of forestry and taxi co-operatives, worker co-operatives are comprised of very small businesses.

5. These co-operatives undertake what we call the "second market of work." The work is often seasonal and may have other uncertainties associated with it.

6. Financing of worker co-operatives differs in the 1980s as opposed to the 1970s. The federal and provincial grants represent but a small part of the financing obtained in the 1980s. Worker co-operatives have sought help from financial institutions, mainly because of loan guarantees from La Société de développement des coopératives, a provincial government agency.

It is important to note that 35 large co-operatives undertake 90 per cent of the total business and have around 40 per cent of the total members. These are the oldest co-operatives (20 are more than 10 years old). They are, by and large, forestry co-operatives which operate in the hinterlands of Québec.

An Analysis of the Contemporary Movement

The current development of worker co-operatives in Québec and Europe is a relatively new social phenomenon which has accompanied the socio-economic and cultural transformations from an industrial to a post-industrial society. An analysis of these transformations is essential for interpreting the growth of worker co-operatives.

Table 8.1

Number of Worker Co-operatives in Various Sectors
of the Economy

	Number	%
Forest and lumber	37	21
Agriculture and food products and blueberry co-operatives	17	10
Diverse manufacturers	24	13
Intellectual and cultural services	24	13
Material services	32	18
Taxi	21	12
Others	23	13
Total	178	100

Post-Industrial Changes

One of the characteristics of this transformation is the inversion in importance of the secondary and tertiary sectors of the economy. White collar workers now form the majority of wage earners. The secondary sector is in a relatively slow decline. The de-industrialization of the Northern countries appears to be an irreversible phenomenon provoked by a series of structural and conjunctural factors. Due to the efforts of trade unions, industrial workers maintained constant pressure for increases in salary which spread to other sectors of the economy. In addition, the harmful effects of industrial production caused the state to assume additional social costs by exercising a heavier tax load on businesses and individuals. With the expansion of international trade, particularly with the newly industrialized countries, and with the two oil crises of the 1970s which multiplied the price of energy, there was a lowering of the total profits of capitalist enterprises. To regain their lost profits, these firms developed the following strategies:

1. shifting industries to the South where the socio-political conditions support higher profits;

2. investing more heavily in labour-saving technologies;

3. getting around collective agreements by reducing the number of permanent employees and replacing them with temporary and part-time workers who have lower salaries, less job security, and poorer working conditions.[12]

These economic upheavals have led to a different type of class conflict, referred to as a "dual society."[13] Workers are divided into two groups with antagonistic interests. On one side, there is a group of wage earners benefitting from job stability, protected social advantages, relatively good pay, and unionization. On the other side, there is an increasing mass of individuals with insecure jobs, predominantly non-unionized, and members of what Gorz called the "non-class," people who are unemployed for an extended period of time.[14] If it is premature to speak of a new class war because there is no class identity, we, nevertheless, observe an increasing gap between these two worlds. There is a paradox which blurs this analysis further: The "traditional" working class can find itself divided between these contradictory interests.

The Social Basis of Labour Co-operation

The emergence of worker co-operatives in Québec can be analyzed in the context of this social transformation. Various social groups are beginning to utilize the co-operative way of work to defend their socio-economic interests. We distinguish four social layers which contain a potential for the creation of worker co-operatives.

The "Traditional" Craftsperson

Traditional craftspersons constituted the majority of members in the French movement prior to the boom in worker co-operatives. They can be found in construction, public works, and printing. In Québec, the labour legislation in construction (the union monopoly on hiring) limited the creation of worker co-operatives in this sector, but the forestry co-operatives have attracted these types of "artisans."

These "free labourers," according to the expression used in the past century, have been hurt by the computer revolution which has dissolved certain jobs. Notably in the printing industry, the typographers -- the labour aristocracy of the past century -- were almost wiped out in one decade.

Workers of the "Weak" Sectors

In 1831, in a labour journal entitled *L'Européen*, Philippe Buchez advocated an association for "free" labourers, carpenters, masons, shoemakers, and locksmiths, "who needed but a few instruments" and "whose ability is the principal capital." But for workers in manufacturing he did not see any possibility to form associations. He proposed for them a special "organization" which he called "syndicat." "By no other means," he explained, "can we displace from the hands of the actual proprietors the capital which makes the fabric."[15]

In fact, Buchez had exclaimed a basic axiom of worker co-operatives -- that each social class develops a type of socio-economic organization which is their own and which corresponds best to the defence of its interests. The labour co-operative was the type of organization for craftspersons, and unions best suited the needs of factory workers. Current industrial changes suggest that the problem is more complex. There are many examples of the closing of factories being prevented by the formation of worker co-operatives. In weak sectors of the economy such as the textile industry the labour co-operative is a means of job maintenance. There are many examples both in Québec and in Europe: the buyout of Tricofil by the FTQ, the LIP adventure in France, the conversion of Manufrance by the CGT, Meridian Motorcycle in England. During the 1970s a new category of worker co-operatives was created that was no longer craft-like but industrial. These factory workers form the most important contingent of new members of worker co-operatives.

The White Collar "Neo-craftspersons"

White collar neo-craftspersons and intellectual workers are another group that is revitalizing the worker co-operative movement. They are in all new trades which treat information like merchandise, the artistic trades, and notably the professionals. In fact this neo-proletariat travels between the exposed and the protected sectors of the economy. Most of the time they are in a marginal work situation and participate in the "non-class" as an active elite and from within conventional organizations and emerging co-operatives. But their individual journey, because of their education which is a privilege, brings them to participate equally in the protected society.

They are the heirs of the blue-collar craftspersons. It is amongst the neo-craftspersons that the co-operative vitality is strongest. They are the ones who animated the self-managed wave of the 1970s and who developed a growing demand for improved quality of life at work and in other endeavours. It is amongst this group that a new culture ferments -- a culture of quality and dignity rather than dependence and a culture of difference rather than normality. These ideals exist even though this class is comparatively privileged. The renaissance of worker co-operatives in Europe during the 1970s is a direct product of the cultural revolution of the 1960s brought forth by students and workers of high professional qualification. This new "salaried elite" is similar to the "labour elite" or craftspersons of the last century. Like the labour elite it is utilizing the worker co-operative as a specific mode of work organization.

The "Non-class"

Finally there exists what Gorz called the "non-class," the new "lumpen proletariat," an increasing mass comprised of structurally unemployed and "marginal" workers. These individuals are unemployed because of their inadequate qualifications (i.e., the graduated neo-proletariat or the functionally illiterate), their "marginal minority" status (women, youth), and their geographical location in economically underdeveloped regions.

This "social layer" is the target of government policies that favour the creation of worker co-operatives as institutions of "social daycare." Because the more disadvantaged of the non-class do not participate in the labour force, their mobilization is very difficult. The emerging socio-economic organizations for people belonging objectively to this "non-class" are, therefore, founded and controlled by the "alternative neo-proletariat" of the "white collar neo-craftspersons."

Under the guidance of the state, a new type of organization emerges out of the non-class. These are human resource co-operatives, "groups of co-operative labour," of which we cannot find any historical example in the industrialized countries, except for the Bracchianti co-operatives and luggage handlers of Italy. Auxi-Plus, a homecare worker co-operative in Montréal, and the temporary manpower co-operatives in Paris are, in fact, protective organizations for marginal workers. This type of co-operative is undoubtedly destined for greater development where it is possible to harmonize the interests of marginal workers and national and multi-national enterprises and, of course, where the co-operatives do not contradict the interests of the unionized workers in the same sector of the economy.

To understand the current rebirth of worker co-operatives in Québec and in other parts of the world, it is necessary to relate the co-operatives to their respective social bases. Each type has specific problems, and there are differences in the types which prevent them from being reduced to a common model. In conclusion to this brief outlook of the social history of worker co-operatives in Québec, it would be hazardous to predict the future. However, it is certain that the small creative "boom" at the beginning of the 1980s is finished. It was linked to unemployment provoked by an economic crisis. What remains are the objective structural conditions which have sustained this rebirth of worker co-operatives. It is probable that this young co-operative sector will continue to develop. As to its rhythm and strength, only time will tell.

Notes

[1]Benoit Levesque *et al.*, *Profil Socio-Économique des Co-opératives de Travail au Québec* (Montréal: Université du Québec and the Comité Provincial des Coopératives de Travail, 1985)

[2]The Québec Federation of Worker Co-operatives has just been recognized by the Co-operative Council of Québec. The Federation's president was elected to the Administrative Council in 1988.

[3]Most of the historical data concerning the nineteenth century is taken from Paul Vincent, *Les Caractéristiques Propres des Coopératives de Travailleurs et leurs Conditions Historique d'Émergence* (Montréal: Centre de Gestion des Coopératives, 1985).

[4]Levesque, *Profil Socio-Économique*.

[5]Claude Carbonneau, "Forestry Co-ops Ring up $180 Million in Sales," *Worker Co-op*, 8, No. 1 (1988), 14.

[6]Raymond Louis, *Les Coopératives de Main-d'Oeuvre: Déclin ou Relance* (Genève: B.I.T., 1982).

[7]The information on Harpell is taken from Paul Vincent, *L'Histoire d'une Communauté Ouvrière et d'une Transformation d'Entreprise en Coop de Travailleurs, L'Imprimerie Coopérative Harpell* (Montréal, Centre de Gestion des Coopératives, 1985).

[8]Centre Coopératif de Recherche en Politique Sociale, "*Les Coopératives de Production et la Lutte des Travailleurs* (Québec: C.E.Q., 1975).

[9]Taxi co-operatives continue to be listed by the state as worker co-operatives. However, their structure more closely resembles agricultural co-operatives.

[10]The history of Tricofil is presented in Paul-André Boucher and Jean-Louis Martel, *Tricofil tel que vécu* (Montréal: Editions C.I.R.I.E.C. et les Presses H.E.C., 1982).

[11]Levesque, *Profil Socio-Économique*.

[12]Pierre Rosanvallon summarizes this logic in *Accumulation du Capital-Contraintes Techno-Économiques* (Paris: Points, 1979), p. 32.

[13]Alain Minc, *Collected Works* (Paris: Gallimard, 1980), p. 187.

[14]Concept developed by A. Gorz in *Adieux au Prolétariat* (Paris: Éditions Galilée, 1980.)

[15]Armand Cuvillier, *Hommes et Idéologies de 1840* (Paris: Marcel Rivière, 1956).

Chapter 9

Worker Co-ops and Community Economic Development

Greg MacLeod

At one time I thought that everything co-operative was good. Later when I was on a visit to Haiti, I met an American businessperson involved in the pharmaceutical industry. In answer to my criticism of American exploitation of the local farmers, he replied that they bought all of their herbs from the Haitian marketing co-operative. Upon further investigation, I was told that there were only five people in that co-operative and one of them was a cabinet minister in the government. Everything can be abused and misconstrued from its original purposes. Nevertheless, this story underlines the importance of going beyond a narrow mechanistic view of worker co-ops to a broader model of economic development.

Concept of a Model

Before going into any detail on the notion of community economic development and how it relates to worker ownership, it is important to discuss what is meant by a model -- the mechanical and the organic. A model is an intellectual pattern or framework that we use to guide us in making things and creating organizations. If we are in the mechanical mode, then we view

175

each particular model as independent, self-contained, and autonomous. The model is fixed, and we must modify the world to fit the model.

By contrast, the organic mode is fluid and changing. Each part is seen as dependent and part of something else. It is dynamic and evolving. Some people would argue that a foot is a foot regardless of whom it is attached to. I would say that each foot is different, depending upon whose foot it is. In a similar vein, it is difficult to assess a worker-owned enterprise as something in itself; it depends upon what it is a part of.

Of course, the conceptual model may be based on a concrete historical case such as Rochdale or Mondragon. If that is so, it is especially important that the model be taken in an organic sense. History does not stop and socio-economic circumstances, especially the state of technology, are in constant flux. Thus, it is important to take models in a very organic sense -- as a jump-off point open to all sorts of modifications and adaptations. A lot will depend upon the climate and the soil. For instance, in an organic model, structural dimensions such as relations between workers and their board of directors are relative, while the principles upon which this relationship is based -- solidarity, sharing, and community are constant and unchanging.

All social and economic activities can only be understood in an organic mode. Traditional economists of both the left and the right have tended to view human reality as mechanical -- as if a shift in the share-capital system were like a shift in the electrical circuitry of a vehicle. To understand socio-economic activity it is not enough to look simply at ownership and flow of capital. In fact, it could be irrelevant as far as the general health of the surrounding society is concerned.

Using the organic model, a worker-owned enterprise can be viewed as a plant. It is a new species, but its significance depends upon the socio-economic environment where it is located. The environment may be too harsh and hostile for the plant to survive, or this new plant may be so strong and aggressive that it will do harm to the rest of the social environment in which it finds itself.

In the organic perspective, everything is attached to

everything else and must be considered in relationship to other elements in the social environment. For instance, we could have a group of carpenters in a small town who are organized as a worker co-operative. If I look at this co-op from the point of view of the worker-members, my perspective may be quite different than the perspective of the general community. If the worker co-op were self-interested, it would charge the highest possible price to build houses and could even monopolize the market in a limited environment. However, the other citizens would view this as bad because the price of housing was unreasonably high.

It makes a vast difference whether one begins from the point of view of making a strong worker-owned enterprise, or whether one begins from the point of view of making a strong local community. In the former case, the community could be a source of resources to make the enterprise strong; in the latter case the worker-owned enterprise is one of the resources in making the local community strong.

Although these distinctions may appear to be "picky," they do make a difference in reality. Thirty or 40 years ago there were a number of co-operative dairies in Nova Scotia. With new technology and the need to centralize, dairies (including the co-ops) began to buy out each other. Today, there is only one co-operative dairy in northern Nova Scotia; there is none on Cape Breton Island. With centralization, the small towns of Cape Breton, like smaller centres in many other regions, lost out in jobs and general economic wealth. From the point of view of a town such as Sydney Mines with unemployment of 30 per cent, this centralization was not good. However, from the point of view of the co-operative dairy, the development was very good because the new enterprise is prospering.

This brings us to the broader question of the general community good, as opposed to the good of a number of particular individuals or even of a number of particular businesses. In the context of the general community good worker ownership is neutral -- neither good nor bad. The shift of ownership of the means of production from non-workers to workers may or may not be more socially responsible. Nevertheless, it can be an important instrument in the process of community economic development. Community economic development is not neutral, it is a value-laden, conscious strategy to promote the general community welfare.

The traditional distinction between "ends and means" is useful in any discussion about community economic development. As an end in themselves, worker co-operatives are not particularly interesting; but as a means for the development of a local community, they are very interesting. They can be a very important piece in a strategy for personal development as well as local development.

Community Economic Development

At this point a clarification of "community economic development" would be useful. Although quite fashionable now, the idea is not new. For generations, social reformers have seen the necessity of harnessing economic institutions to the more noble motive of human improvement. The majority of founders of the co-operative movement saw the co-operative as a part of a broad movement for social improvement rather than as an instrument for personal benefit of a small minority. As Melnyk has pointed out, most co-operatives have moved into the institutional mode and concentrated on economic survival while neglecting the other dimensions of the original movement.[1] Indeed this may have been necessary; if co-ops had not concentrated on the purely economic, there would be few left in Canada today. Good will and good intentions are not enough to enable survival in the cruel, hard world of market economics.

During the sixties, people who were most concerned with social reform and humanistic development were not particularly interested in the commercial world of economic development. Indeed there was a certain amount of aversion for budgets and efficiency. Among many activists in the community movements, this aversion extended to co-operatives. Though it is somewhat of a caricature, one could almost say that the major co-operative enterprises as a group, and the various organizations for social reform of the sixties, remained quite apart from each other and even distrustful of each other. The term "community economic development" may well represent a synthesis of these distinct social movements. This term represents the attempt to unite many of the ideals of the sixties, for example, democratic sharing and solidarity of all people in a local community, with the effective commercial instruments developed in the co-operative sector.

Development

Many of the movements in the sixties represented a reflection of the reigning notions of "development" which were destructive of a full life. Both capitalist as well as socialist business activities tended to concentrate on only material development -- more and more production with less and less social development. A preferable notion of development, which is based upon more ancient sources, comes from Aristotle. For Aristotle every person as well as every community has unfulfilled capacities. The purpose of life is to fulfill these capacities, that is, to grow. It is not easy to discern what these capacities are and it takes a lot of critical reflection. However, it is clear that life on the personal as well as the social level concerns figuring out what we are and what we could be.

In this sense, development is about growth, about the fulfillment of capacities. Outsiders can help, but this kind of development can only happen from inside -- both on the personal and community level. Resources, both material and human, can be regarded as opportunities for fulfillment. Depleted communities, characterized by high unemployment and socio-economic depression, are that way not because resources are absent, but rather because of a lack of enabling structures. By enabling structures, I mean institutions of a political or economic nature which allow people to achieve their purposes. People in every community have needs, or unfulfilled capacities, and require institutions to fulfill them.

For Don José María Arizmendia-Arrieta, the founder of the Mondragon experiment in the Basque country of Spain, there are three types of organizations which should be the key instruments in the establishment of a renewed and better social order: co-operative, labour, and political parties. Each of these organizations is relatively independent but is also based upon complementary principles. Indeed there would be no lasting social reform, in his view, unless there was success on these three fronts. The key question is how worker co-ops can serve as one of these enabling institutions. In one key area, they are especially appropriate -- the area of control.

Ownership vs. Control

In his classic work on company law, L.C.B. Gower points out that the key issue in the business world is not ownership but control.[2] Large modern corporations, whether owned in a capitalistic mode or a co-operative mode, are controlled by management. Management is highly sophisticated and technocratic. Indeed, modern businesses could not function without sophisticated managers because the legal owners are usually incapable of understanding the complicated issues.

Economically depleted communities are characterized by a lack of enabling institutions and by a lack of competent managers. Universities train the children of poor communities to move on to centres of affluence where they can "get ahead." Most universities do not encourage their leading students to return to their communities to serve as managers for local businesses. In desperation, depleted communities welcome outside industries, but this is for survival and not development. Proper development comes through local control and local management.

When development is locally controlled, it is more likely to be in accord with local tradition. Community members and their children live with the results of their economic decisions -- distant managers do not. This is not to attribute malice or hard-heartedness to distant managers; distance itself is simply an impediment to understanding the local scene.

With the loss of local control and local capacity, much energy is spent in chasing after outside authorities for a share in the abundance evident in the main capital cities. The native communities of Canada are especially aware of this reality. They have opted for more local control even though more "mistakes" will be made. After all, communities can learn to be autonomous and mature only through being permitted to make mistakes -- the way an individual does.

Ownership is relevant only insofar as it permits local control. By its nature, development of the local community means a growing self-sufficiency. The more the local community can do for itself on all levels, cultural as well as economic, then the better off it is. This sense of development promotes growth and independence.

Community

Just because we all belong to one nation or even one province does not mean that we are one community. I take community in a living sense. I refer to a group of people living in a definite geographic area who regard themselves as sharing some kind of identity. This is more a sociological reality than an economic one. The French use the term "pays." When they began closing the mines in the south of France, the miners demonstrated with the cry that they wanted to live and work in their own "pays" and not move to the north of France. Again, the notion of an organic unity as opposed to a mechanical unity is useful here. A community is a growing reality; it is people living and working together and sharing common histories. It cannot be defined in quantitative terms such as the size of the territory or the number of inhabitants. Music and literature usually express the character of a community. This sort of description is extremely frustrating for administrators and technically-oriented officials.

In many parts of the world traditional communities have been reorganized and divided according to the external needs of more powerful economic and political systems. The weaker communities have not been able to organize their own economic and political structures, whether it is in old Europe with the Irish and Basque "problems" or in the political patchwork of Africa. On a smaller and more modest scale we have these tensions in North America. Besides the dramatic dilemmas of the native populations, we have many other smaller, traditional communities which cannot survive as social and cultural entities. The Canadian government has been especially generous with mobility allowances to encourage the hinterland unemployed to migrate to the larger centres. But, of course, this "solution" means destruction of the traditional communities and not their development.

In non-metropolitan areas, community groups can constitute agents of development; they can set up economic instruments which operate on behalf of the community. This kind of communal belonging is much more difficult to find in large metropolitan centres. Interestingly enough, within the metropolitan areas it appears that communal identity survives best in the most disfavoured areas -- the ghettos and inner cities.

These claims about community are debatable. In the conventional economic perspective, which is mechanistic, the reality of "community" is external. It does not enter into the plans for economic change; it is difficult to fit into an econometric model. However, by shifting our paradigm to an organic model, communal reality becomes a key issue. It is important how the commercial life affects social and cultural lives of people. In fact, these latter elements can become resources and sources for economic development.

Economic

By now it should be clear that I do not accept the conventional notion of economics. Like so many other sciences developed in the nineteenth century, economics is in need of radical reforms. Most of the formulas and explanations proposed by economists during this generation have not been very helpful. In this I am not saying anything new; many members of the economics' profession are saying so.[3]

The Oxford concise dictionary defines "economy" as the "administration of concerns and resources of a community."

Economic activity is concerned with the management of scarce resources "in a particular community." Because economics concerns the resources of the community, it should be controlled by the community and directed for its benefit.

A notion of economic activity which detaches economics from the community is unacceptable. For example, in an abstract economic system, there would be an economic improvement if all of the fishing were carried on by three or four factory trawlers off the coast of Nova Scotia with all of the fish being landed in Lunenburg. The gross product would increase; more efficient machines with fewer workers would result in increased profit going to a number of prominent Nova Scotian families. Yet the many fishing villages of Nova Scotia would be finished. This would not be economic development for these villages. I insist upon a notion of economic activity which is always connected with a specific community. It is not necessarily so, but it could be that the good of a half-dozen families could be different from the good of a dozen fishing villages. What if an American company were to offer each of the concerned families a half-billion dollars for their share of the fishing industry -- the deal is made -- and then the factory trawlers land their fish in Boston!

Joan Robinson, the Cambridge economist, claims that all economic theory can be boiled down to moral theory.[4] Economic activity is about human activity and hence necessarily involves moral decisions. The movement for community economic development attempts to relate all economic decisions to the larger context of human and social development. Economic growth in a country or in a province does not mean that people are better off economically. Sometimes the growth is concentrated within a small minority of wealthy individuals or in one capital city while other groups and other subregions suffer. Also, prosperity in one business enterprise does not mean that the community as a community is better off.

More and more people in the industrialized world are realizing that the concept of a worker-owned enterprise, or any kind of a business enterprise (capitalist or co-operative), is not adequate in itself. It can be evaluated only in relation to the larger issues of community economic development. A worker-owned enterprise is suitable as part of and integral to larger commercial structures in a local community. The danger is that the workers will think that the wealth generated belongs to them alone. Especially in a modern technological society it is evident that increased productivity depends in large measure upon the technology used. Science and technology are the fruits of the total society and of generations past. The general community and not simply the employees of an enterprise has a claim on the wealth produced.

If a worker-owned enterprise is to follow the principles of community economic development, then it must collaborate with other commercial institutions sharing the same principles. For example, it must collaborate with the local credit union, use its resources to establish new enterprises for the less fortunate, and in general act for the good of the total community and not simply for its own employees.

Mondragon

One of the best models for community economic development is the Mondragon experiment.[5] It is called an "experiment" because it is not finished; perhaps it will never be finished.

The Mondragon co-operative experiment began in 1956. Thirty years later, it is the largest and most impressive co-operative industrial complex in the world with annual sales of approximately $2 billion. In 1985, Mondragon had over 170 co-operatives and employed almost 19,000 workers, mainly in the industrial enterprises. The movement includes its own research centre for the humanization of work, its own social-security system, and its own co-operative bank or credit union, The Caja Laboral.

The whole complex can be divided into three major divisions: 1) associated co-operatives of which there are 167; 2) the Workers' Credit Union or co-operative bank; and 3) support bodies of which there are six. The associated co-operatives may be broken down into three subdivisions: industrial sector, agricultural and consumer sector, and educational and housing. The majority of the associated co-operatives are involved in heavy and technical industry.

The Co-operative Bank (Credit Union)

Leaders in the Mondragon system freely admit today that if they did not have their own banking system, there would be no worker co-operatives in their community. They cannot imagine a serious producer co-operative system without an associated bank. Throughout the years of the economic crisis in Spain, the Mondragon system survived while many traditional companies went bankrupt.

The role of the Caja was clear from the beginning. It was meant to entrap local financial resources and invest them in the creation of new enterprises for the development of the Basque region, which was suffering from high unemployment. People in a local village were told very plainly that deposits in the credit union would create new businesses and jobs for their children. The motto was "suitcases or savings books." The total customer deposits in 1986 amounted to $1.7 billion. It operated with two distinct divisions: Financial and Entrepreneurial. Today each division is legally separate with its own board of directors. The Entrepreneurial Division is now one of the "Support Bodies."

Support Bodies

In general the support bodies are second-level co-operatives. Their role is to promote, assist, and develop new and existing producer co-operatives. As second-level organizations, their boards are hybrid, always involving the employees as well as those they serve. This is to avoid the double possibility of the producer exploiting the consumer or the consumer exploiting the producer. There are six such bodies: the League of Education and Culture, Ikerlan Research Centre, Iksabide Management Development Centre, Lankide Export Agency, Lagun Aro Social Security, and the Entrepreneurial Division.

Entrepreneurial Division

This enterprise resembles a combined chartered accounting and technical-consulting company. Its functions are threefold: 1) to develop new co-operative enterprises; 2) to provide technical consulting assistance to members; and 3) to audit and monitor the financial operations of all members. Because the Caja was founded with the specific purpose of capturing local capital for the creation of new enterprises, the entrepreneurial division developed as a natural correlate. The accumulated capital would not do much good unless there were structures to put the capital to work.

At present, the Mondragon system is not able to absorb all of the capital available through the Caja, so approximately 65 per cent is invested in conventional securities. The Entrepreneurial Division is a support and nerve centre for the total Mondragon complex. One-third of its board members represents the Credit Union, one-third represents the Group Council of Producer co-operatives, and one-third represents its own employees. The Entrepreneurial Division is divided into the following three departments:

Economic Analysis -- This department studies national and international trends especially at the macro-economic level. At least five years before Spain entered the Common Market, the Economic Analysis Department had been analyzing the Common Market's impact upon Mondragon enterprises. It issues regular reports on various aspects of the Basque economy. At the present time it is studying the world economy to pinpoint four or five dynamic areas.

Agricultural and Food Promotion -- Its objective is to provide necessary technical and entrepreneurial assistance to agricultural enterprises. An attempt is made to apply the principles which have been successful in the secondary industry to agriculture. The effects of integration and modern technology are striking. Near the Lenniz furniture factory, there is a sawmill which is connected by conveyer belts. The timber arrives, is milled, and then passed next door into an ultra-modern factory system which is programmed by computer. Retail customers in department stores choose a model for their kitchen. The order is immediately transmitted to the factory which operates on a modular system, turning out with the same machines a wide variety in style and colour. Crates of furniture are automatically stacked at loading portals. When there is a sufficient load for a particular town or city, then it is delivered. There is little inventory. All of this is a result of linking forest production to the retail market by using planning and technology.

Industrial Promotion -- This department is responsible for

the initiation of new industrial co-operatives. It identifies
products and tests their feasibility. It is always in search of
new ideas in countries such as Japan, Germany, France, and
the USA. Its agents gather once a year to discuss ideas for
new product development.

In a typical month, about 30 proposals are analyzed. The
department uses a filtering process to develop a short list of about
10 per cent of the originals. Then one product is selected for a
preliminary feasibility study. If the indicators are positive the
process will continue in a most interesting manner. Before a
full-scale feasibility study is begun, two key people are appointed:
a prospective manager and an advisor or 'godfather.' If the
feasibility study is positive, the implementation process is begun.
First, the Board of the Caja must approve the business plan for
financial support. Then the manager recruits a technical team
from within the system and a new co-operative is incorporated.

An example will help to clarify the process. A few years ago a
market gap was identified in the field of forklifts. After a positive
feasibility, an arrangement was made to purchase a
manufacturing license from Mitsubishi through their agent in
Japan. A new co-operative called Oinakar was incorporated. In
the usual cautious manner, the co-operative began by assembling
components purchased from Mitsubishi. If the enterprise is
profitable, it will manufacture the complete product. An advisor
was assigned to monitor the company for two years on behalf of
the department.

The cost of development was approximately $60,000. Of this,
the Basque government paid 40 per cent and the rest was
assigned as a long-term loan to the new enterprise.
Approximately 35 workers constitute the membership and they
contributed $330,000 in capitalization or approximately $9,000
per worker. The Caja provided a $1.5 million loan. Another
$500,000 was provided by the Basque government. Sales for
Oinakar in 1987 were approximately $6 million.

No part of the Mondragon experimental complex exists on its
own. It is an organic network of parts and pieces with roots deep
in the local community, which nourish and support each other.
That philosophy is exportable, though the mechanical bits and
pieces of the system may not be.

New Dawn

Another model of organic development is New Dawn in Cape Breton, Nova Scotia. From a financial point of view, it is not even close to the Mondragon league; its assets are in the order of $10 million. Nevertheless, New Dawn demonstrates that it is possible for a group of citizens to control and develop economic resources for the good of their community rather than for private interests.

Again, an enterprise like New Dawn must be regarded as an experiment. The structures are not ideologically based and they are in flux. Conventional economic theory contends that the motor of all wealth creation is the increase of individual profit. New Dawn departs from this principle in that the principal beneficiary is the community; benefits to the participants come from their participation in the community.

New Dawn was started in the early seventies by a dozen do-gooders searching for a project that would make at least a modest contribution to their community. Most of the founders were part of the local co-operative movement and were frustrated by a great deal of talk and not enough action. From the beginning, their concept was multi-functional: If one business got going, then that could be a building block for something else.

The first undertaking was the purchase of an old commercial building. Some of the board members guaranteed a loan for the down payment and a mortgage was obtained from League Savings. The second floor was converted into apartments while the bottom was used for a handicraft centre as well as conventional commercial rentals. The loan was soon repaid and the building became self-financing. New Dawn built on this base, buying other properties and renting them.

As time went on New Dawn simply responded to needs. A small guest home for senior citizens was established in Whitney Pier. This unit employs about a dozen workers who are unionized. Many local groups had been complaining about the lack of dentists; people either had to wait over a year for an appointment or travel to Halifax. New Dawn built several dental facilities and brought in dentists through attractive lease-purchase arrangements. New Dawn has tried a variety of business enterprises. Some were successful and some were not. Although New Dawn can survive on its present asset base, mainly real estate, the intention is to expand and to establish any new business that improves the community and is also profitable. Even though the structure is not-for-profit, an attempt is made to generate revenue for re-investment in the community.

New Dawn is self-sustaining, though much of the present activity depends upon a variety of government programs. This is not bad because government needs partners at the community level if it is to meet its social and economic responsibilities. It is unfortunate that often the partners available to government are multi-nationals. Perhaps, in the future, the co-operative community-based business sector will be able to play a much greater role in collaborating with government.

Others

Communities are most inventive when they are threatened with extinction. In this generation, the industrial areas of Scotland have been devastated by unemployment of around 40 per cent. As in Canada, there have been a variety of government make-work schemes. Strathclyde is one example where community groups are attempting to utilize some of these programs in a creative way to establish businesses which will benefit the local area. The umbrella organization is called "Strathclyde Community Business Limited," a not-for-profit corporation that acts as a generator and resource centre for new businesses. The new enterprises are small; some are employee-owned and some are individually-owned. Examples are a window-washing company, a restaurant, a security firm, etc. The Strathclyde group offers this definition to explain what it is about:

> A community business is a trading organization which is set up, owned and controlled by the local community and which aims to create ultimately self-supporting jobs for local people and be a focus for local development. Any profits made from its business activities go either to create more employment or to provide local services, or to assist other schemes of community benefit.[6]

Many of the states in the southern United States have suffered from the vagaries of the American economy. In the coal regions of Appalachia, the 1984 unemployment rate ranged from 14 to 18 per cent. On behalf of the organization called "Southerners for Economic Justice," Steve Fisher presents a view of economics which is defined by community needs:

> Development in the south can best be defined as the process by which the region's residents make the economy better serve their fundamental needs. These include:
>
> • The right to meaningful work that is not life threatening either in the short or long term. This right implies both a safe workplace and a safe environment.
>
> • The right to economic security, both in terms of job security and equitable remuneration for work done. This remuneration should be sufficient to ensure decent housing, healthcare, etc.
>
> • The right to participate as fully as possible in any decision-making affecting their livelihoods, i.e., democratic control of the workplace.
>
> • The right to preservation of cultural integrity. Economic development should not destroy the cultural integrity of the people for whom the development is taking place.[7]

In an Austrian village, a group of farmers set up a wood-chip heating plant for their community while another group has established an herb packaging and marketing company to add a bit of extra income to their marginal farms. In many rural areas of the industrialized world, community groups have established tourist businesses to strengthen their economic base. In all of these cases, the line between private and public has become blurred. Outside of Mondragon, the examples are not of a large scale. Certainly in France and Italy there are large and successful worker co-operatives which have been widely reported. Between 1978 and 1983 the number of workers in producer co-operatives increased from 190,000 to 540,000.[8] Many of these were formed by workers taking over a failing industry. Canada has much to learn from them.

The cases with which I am concerned go beyond the survival or enhancement of a particular industry. They involve the survival of the community in general. It is true that sometimes the end of an industry means the end of a community. Nevertheless, even a one-industry approach can make a difference to the development of a community.

Smaller communities have become highly vulnerable in our economic system because governments provide generous allowances for labour mobility. If existing communities are valuable and worth preserving, a great deal more imagination as well as political will is required. Rather than being a technique, community economic development is a philosophy of development which entails solidarity, local responsibility, and creativity. In themselves, worker co-ops are a mechanical technique; whether they partake of a wider community purpose or not depends upon the philosophy of the participants.

Notes

[1]George Melnyk, *The Search for Community* (Montréal: Black Rose, 1985).

[2]L.C.B. Gower, *The Principles of Modern Company Law* (London: Steven & Sons, 1969).

[3]E.F. Schumacher, *Small is Beautiful* (New York: Harper & Row, 1973); and John K. Galbraith, *The New Industrial State* (Boston: Haughton, 1967).

[4]Joan Robinson, *An Essay on Marxian Economics* (London: MacMillan, 1972), p. 8.

[5]José Azurmendi, *El Hombre Co-opertiva* (Mondragon: Caja Laboral Popular, 1986); and José María Arizmendi-Arrieta, *Collected Writings* (Sydney: University of Cape Breton Archives, Unpublished).

[6]*Strathclyde Community Business Annual Report* (Glasgow: Govan, 1988), p. 4.

[7]Steve Fisher, *Everybody's Business*, XIV, No. 5-6, p. 7.

[8]Robert Oakeshott, *The Case for Workers' Co-ops* (London: Routledge & Kegan Paul, 1978), Ch. 8-9.

Chapter 10

Future Directions
for Worker Ownership: A Postscript

George Melnyk

In the economies of the world, whether they be capitalist or socialist, there exists a basic division between the employee and the employer, no matter who the employer is -- individual conglomerate, or the state. Likewise, there exists a fundamental separation between workers, who do as they are told, and management that tells them what to do.

This traditional state of affairs has meant that the ideas of worker ownership and self-management have been generally greeted with at least skepticism, if not outright hostility, on the part of both employers and employees. Workers are not accustomed to such a situation and managers consider it a threat to their prerogatives and expertise. The implications of worker ownership and the amalgamation of roles which it entails are very serious for any hierarchically-structured system. Worker ownership unnerves both the capitalist and the commissar.

The roots of the worker-ownership concept are found in early nineteenth-century European history with such thinkers as Robert Owen (1771-1858), Charles Fourier (1772-1837), and P.J. Proudhon (1809-1865). The concept arose with the development of an industrial working class, and it was based in the democratic tendencies unleased by the French Revolution and the socialist critique of capitalism that became widespread during that century.[1]

However, neither the socialist nor the co-operative movements that came into their own during this period made worker ownership a key feature. Socialism split into three main streams: the social democratic, the communist, and the anarchist. Social democracy found its apog´ee in trade unionism; communism found its strength in the dictatorship of the proletariat through the state; and anarchism, which was most favourable to direct worker ownership, found itself with insufficient political acceptance. During the Spanish Civil War, the anarcho-syndicalist movement was able to institute worker ownership and control but this lasted only for a brief time.

The co-operative movement, especially in the Anglophone world, turned its attention toward consumer and producer co-ops and away from worker co-ops, resulting in that component being the smallest element in the International Co-operative Alliance. The worker-ownership concept has split into two main streams. The first is direct worker ownership, which refers to all forms of direct worker participation in the ownership and operation of a particular enterprise. The second refers to all forms of indirect or mediated worker ownership in which there is a second party that claims ownership and management on behalf of the workers in the enterprise. An example would be the enterprises owned by the Israeli labour movement, the Histadrut.

This book has focused on the direct stream and, in particular, its co-operative component. This focus has allowed an evaluation of the achievements and failures of this component with the result that we can now begin to understand what restrictions the movement faces and what are its realistic possibilities for the future.

The minority status of direct worker ownership has resulted from two fundamental factors -- the first internal to the idea of worker ownership and the second external to it. The internal restriction comes from the high principles which direct worker ownership entails. These principles include:

1. democratic decision-making in production;

2. restrictions on the hierarchical mode of ownership and organization;

3. workers' self-management;

4. the priority of labour over capital; and

5. worker ownership's competitiveness in private- and public-sector dominated economies.

The view of human nature which these principles express is a high-minded one and one which most societies have traditionally rejected. Even in Communist Party-controlled states, whose official ideology is worker-oriented, the average worker has low status. While in capitalist societies the class structure is such that the workers are viewed as incapable of being anything else but cogs in a production process. The anti-elitism of direct worker ownership means that each individual worker is viewed as a self-determining person capable of sound decision-making for the overall good of an enterprise.

The second factor that inhibits the spread of worker ownership is the strength of the forces aligned against it and the weakness of the forces that support it. Opposed to worker ownership as a dominant mode of economic organization are a variety of entrenched ideologies of both the left and the right as well as institutions of the state, business, and labour, who view worker ownership as a threat to the status quo. There are customary ways of viewing the organization of work to which citizens around the world have been socialized. These forces tolerate in varying degrees a minority status for direct worker ownership and management, as long as worker ownership does not mean a fundamental restructuring of relations for socio-economic organization.

The weakness of the forces supporting worker ownership only enhances the power of the opposition. The co-operative movement, which is committed to democratic ownership, does not dominate the economy in any country. Canada, which has a relatively strong co-operative sector, currently generates fewer than 100 new worker co-op businesses annually, while the private sector is generating up to 10,000 new businesses monthly.[2] In the United States nearly 9 million workers are enrolled in employee-ownership plans, most of which provide an indirect and limited form of worker participation and control, and which in no way challenges the prerogatives of a capitalist-driven economy.[3] The forces promoting an enhanced form of direct worker ownership and local control are small, regional groups without significant national impact.[4]

In spite of the problems associated with realizing high principles and the opposition of the status quo, the worker-ownership phenomenon has been expanding rapidly since the 1970s. Avner Ben-Ner of the University of Minnesota calls its worldwide growth "remarkable," while Constance Mungall, a writer on worker co-op development in Canada, points out that the number of worker co-ops in this country has "nearly doubled in just the past five years."[5] However, the fact that direct worker ownership has been so small in the past has meant that it has a long way to go to achieve a substantial presence in the economy.

In the socialist economies of Eastern Europe, worker co-operatives have an increasing acceptance. In Poland there are half a million workers in worker co-ops while in the Soviet Union the recent drive for *perestroika* has resulted in thousands of co-operatively-owned enterprises.[6] Nevertheless, these developments have not changed the minority status of direct worker ownership and management in either socialist or capitalist economies. The situation in Yugoslavia, with its official ideology of worker self-management, is slightly different in that for some time, there has been enterprise self-management but under firm state leadership and control. One can argue that Yugoslavia's self-management system is a socialist version of the American employee share-ownership plan with its heavy restrictions on workers' self-determination and, therefore, does not refute the minority status of direct worker ownership in world economies.

There are three mega-trends which will have an impact on worker ownership -- the new computer-driven technology, the international division of labour especially in manufacturing, and the increasing importance of the tertiary or service sector to employment. The new technology has created a form of industrialization which has modified the workplace and the skills of workers. New businesses have arisen in this environment in increasing numbers, and this has created a space in which the social entrepreneurship associated with worker ownership can flourish. At the same time, capitalism's retreat from traditional industries has resulted in more possibilities for worker takeovers or buyouts. In short, technological innovation provides a climate conducive to increased levels of worker ownership.

The trend toward off-shore manufacturing in Third World countries has added to change already being wrought by the computer revolution. The globalization of production and trade spearheaded by the multi-nationals is now an accepted fact. This means that the mass market is dominated by globalized production, but specialty production in national economies is still viable and an area open to worker ownership. It is in this area that the greatest possibilities exist.

Finally, the almost exponential growth of the third or service sector of the economy in advanced capitalist countries creates further opportunities for employee ownership. The service sector is an area that is not capital intensive. While it may take $100,000 to create a new manufacturing job, it takes only a few thousand to start one in a yardcare business. This is most important for workers for whom capital funds are a real problem.

These three mega-trends offer a measure of optimism for the future of direct worker ownership. That does not mean that worker ownership is somehow the wave of the future. The many problems inherent in worker ownership as outlined in this book preclude such a development in the near future. What will occur is a movement that varies from country to country, so that no two countries will have a similar worker-ownership profile. The reason for this is the determining power of a nation's industrial culture and tradition. Worker ownership is not a monolithic international ideology. It is an outgrowth of and an adaptation to certain conditions. For example, the weakness of the American co-operative movement vis-a-vis that country's capitalism has resulted in an ESOP-dominated form of worker ownership, while in Canada a relatively stronger co-op sector has resulted in the worker co-op option being more accepted. In Germany worker ownership has been tied to a "co-determination" model of management that has come from a powerful trade-union movement and an influential social-democratic party.

The movement for worker ownership does not operate in isolation; it is always tied to a partner that is established and has decided to promote the idea and the practice. When this partner, be it government, trade union movement, the co-op sector, or even elements of the private sector, decides to support worker ownership, it does so in a way that reflects its own interests. And of course, the constellation of power groups and their relationships vary between countries thereby generating a variety of worker-ownership models.

These models are compromises between the interests that are promoting them and the ideals of the worker-ownership concept. In every case worker ownership has a dominant partner (e.g., the state in Yugoslavia, business in the U.S., the co-op sector or provincial governments in Canada), which means that the worker-ownership model prevalent in any political jurisdiction will reflect the interests of that partner more so than the ideals of worker ownership and control. This is the reality of worker ownership as it enters the twenty-first century.

One must not be alarmed by this. The dominant partner exists as the engine of growth for worker ownership because the concept itself has proven insufficient to generate its own substantive dynamism. It is like a sidecar waiting to be attached to a motorcycle before it can go anywhere, but once it is attached it gives the motorcycle a whole new profile. Without the support and encouragement of some major element of the status quo, worker ownership cannot become a popular option for workers. Even in the case of Mondragon, which is considered a self-generated model, the importance of the religious sanction provided by its founder cannot be discounted.[7]

With this situation in mind, a worker-ownership movement has to be clear about its values and its purpose. Otherwise, the results can be negative and counterproductive. When reasons such as job creation, regional economic development, local control, etc., are brought out in support of worker ownership, it is easy to forget that the goal of worker ownership is social and economic advancement for the individual through enhanced personal authority and responsibility. Without this vision, worker ownership can fail to serve the needs of workers and even result in a deterioration of their situation.

The creation of a self-managed and economically successful social sector in which workers feel they have solid financial returns, greater dignity, and participation in a viable future for themselves and their children is the only goal worthy of worker ownership. Models that retain that basic purpose are models of which to be proud.

The essays in this book have provided insight into the process by which a worker co-operative movement comes about, especially in the Canadian context, but the lessons learned here are useful in other environments. The manner in which the Canadian worker co-op movement has grown is simply an example of factors that are widespread. When compared to worker co-op developments in the U.K. or in continental Europe, where certain sectors of the economy have greater concentrations of worker ownership, the Canadian experience has been similar. In the Canadian case it is in the forestry and wood-products industry in which many worker co-ops are located. The sectors will vary from country to country, but predominance in particular economic sectors is characteristic in all countries.

The issues discussed in this book are common to worker ownership wherever it is located, although the stage of the movement may vary from country to country. Just because the worker co-ops of the Mondragon group have solved the perennial problem of capital and Canadian worker co-ops have not, does not mean that other issues such as governance have been handled any better at Mondragon than at a worker-owned and operated sawmill in British Columbia.

For worker ownership to succeed requires that it overcome the structural barriers in its path, both internal and external ones, and that it also provide a better option for the workplace. It does that by remaining true to its vision of the worker as a self-determining individual who finds fulfillment in worker ownership and control.

Notes

[1]For a more detailed discussion see G. Melnyk, "Lessons from the Past: The Tension Between Worker and Consumer Co-operatives in 19th Century Britain," *Worker Co-op*, 4, No. 4 (1986); and Henri Desroche, *Le Project Coopératif* (Paris: Les Editions Ouvrieres, 1976).

[2]*Calgary Herald*, Oct. 17, 1988, p. F3.

[3]"ESOP Growth Strong in 1987," *The Employee Ownership Report*, VIII, No. 5 (1988), 1.

[4]See R. Jackall and H. Levin, eds., *Worker Co-operatives in America* (Berkeley: University of California Press, 1984).

[5]Avner Ben-Ner, "Comparative Empirical Observations on Worker-Owned and Capitalist Firms," *International Journal of Industrial Organization*, 6 (1988), pp. 7-31; and Constance Mungall, *More than Just a Job: Worker Co-operatives in Canada* (Ottawa: Steel Rail, 1986), p. 1.

[6]Bob Schutte "Worker Co-ops in the 1980s" *The Ecumenist*, 23, No.5 (1985); and J. Quarter, "Worker Co-ops Mushrooming in Soviet Economy," *Worker Co-op*, 8, No. 1 (1988).

[7]Jesus Larranaga and Don José María Arizmendi-Arrieta, *La Experiencia Cooperativa de Mondragon* (Mondragon: Caja Laboral Popular, 1981).

Biographies

Gregory Baum is professor of religious studies at McGill University in Montreal. He is a leading Catholic theologian and the author of numerous books.

Alain Brideault is a lecturer at the University of Sherbooke who teaches and has written extensively about worker co-operatives. He is also vice-president of Orion, a worker co-op research company, and on the board of directors of the Comite provincial des cooperatives de travail.

Judith Brown is a doctoral student at The Ontario Institute for Studies in Education. Her master's thesis was about work for the psychiatrically disabled, and her doctoral dissertation is a study of worker participation in co-operative daycare.

Jo-Ann Hannah is a doctoral student at The Ontario Institute for Studies in Education. She has written articles for the *Worker Co-op* magazine and co-authored *Co-operative Entrepreneurship*, a curriculum unit on worker co-operatives for secondary schools.

John E. Jordan is senior vice-president of planning and development at The Co-operators Group Limited. In addition to working for co-operatives for many years, he has written extensively on co-ops and has taught co-operation, management, and planning at York University.

Ginette Lafrenière is a graduate student at the University of Sherbrooke who is focusing on the study of co-operatives.

Greg MacLeod is a professor of philosophy at the University College of Cape Breton, Nova Scotia. He is well-known as a community organizer and theorist. His latest book is *New Age Business: Community Corporations that Work*.

George Melnyk is a writer living in Calgary and an activist in the worker co-op movement. He is author of *Radical Regionalism* and *The Search for Community*.

Jack Quarter is a professor of community psychology at The Ontario Institute for Studies in Education. He is the author of numerous books and articles on education and psychology and editor of the *Worker Co-op* magazine.

WHEN FREEDOM WAS LOST
The Unemployed, the Agitator, and the State
by Lorne Brown

An examination of an important chapter in Canadian history, the 1930's when thousands of unemployed men were forced into work camps and subjected to poor living conditions, slave wages, and military discipline.

Lorne Brown seeks to remedy the dearth of the 30's labour Canadiana with this study of little-known labour camps.
Books in Canada
208 pages, photographs
Paperback ISBN: 0-920057-77-2 $14.95
Hardcover ISBN: 0-920057-75-6 $34.95

THE POLITICS OF HUMAN SERVICES
by Steven Wineman

A scathing personal and political account of Wineman's experience as a welfare worker, offering a concrete, detailed plan for wholesale conversion of existing human services programmes. His strategy for "radical decentralisation" combines the struggles of oppressed and marginalized groups in an integrated movement for change. He envisions businesses, housing, health care and support networks that are democratically run, co-operatively managed and controlled by the people who use them.

Wineman makes a strong case against capitalism and the welfare state.
Books in Canada
272 pages
Paperback ISBN: 0-920057-43-8 $14.95
Hardcover ISBN: 0-920057-42-X $29.95

THE SEARCH FOR COMMUNITY
From Utopia to a Co-operative Society
by George Melnyk

Co-ops in capitalist and communist nations alike are assessed for strengths and drawbacks as he selects the components that can be adapted to our society and used to link groups already functioning. The result is the "social co-operative," a new citizen-run structure that will successfully respond to our social and economic requirements.

Melnyk offers a fascinating social history of co-operatives, from monastery to commune.
Choice
170 pages
Paperback ISBN: 0-920057-52-7 $9.95
Hardcover ISBN: 0-920057-53-5 $29.95

THE ANARCHIST COLLECTIVES
Workers' Self-Management in Spain 1936-39
edited by Sam Dolgoff
A definitive collection of analyses on the radical collectives organised in Spain, with an introduction by Murray Bookchin.

The eyewitness reports and commentary presented in this highly important study reveal a very different understanding of the nature of socialism and the means for achieving it.
Noam Chomsky
195 pages, illustrated
Paperback ISBN: 0-919618-20-0 $14.95
Hardcover ISBN: 0-919618-21-9 $29.95

DURRUTI
The People Armed
by Abel Paz
translated by Nancy MacDonald
An exhaustive biography of the legendary Spanish revolutionary Buenaventura Durruti, who died at age forty in 1936. Durruti was an uncompromising anarchist who knew battle, exile, imprisonment, strikes, insurrections and life underground. This man, who started life as a rebellious young worker and who at his death was mourned by millions, acted always on the conviction that freedom and revolution are inseparable, refusing all honours, awards and bureaucratic positions.

Wherever you go it's Durruti and Durruti again, whom you hear spoken of as a wonder man.
Toronto **Daily Star**
323 pages, illustrated
Paperback ISBN: 0-919618-74-X $14.95
Hardcover ISBN: 0-919618-73-1 $29.95

THE HISTORY OF THE LABOUR MOVEMENT IN QUÉBEC
by the Education Committees of the CSN and CEQ
translated by Arnold Bennett
In each of nine chapters, a well-known Québec writer analyses a particular period in the 150-year history of Québec unions.

Convey[s] an impressive body of knowledge about the Québec labour movement, working class conditions and working class struggles. A first-rate historical analysis of the Québec union movement...insightful and well-informed.
McGill Daily
304 pages
Paperback ISBN: 0-920057-56-X $19.95
Hardcover ISBN: 0-920057-55-1 $39.95

DEMOCRACY AND THE WORK PLACE
by Harold B. Wilson
2nd edition

Wilson goes beyond the philosophical to show how industrial democracy can be achieved.
Toronto **Star**

Even though they might not like what they read, corporate managers should run out and buy a copy.
Vancouver **Sun**
155 pages
Paperback ISBN: 0-919618-22-7 $9.95
Hardcover ISBN: 0-919618-23-5 $19.95

QUÉBEC LABOUR
Preface by Marcel Pépin
2nd revised edition

Marcel Pépin is former president of the CNTU, or Confederation of National Trade Unions, a major force in Québec's labour history. He provides a lively introduction to this definitive account of its development and unique features: its origins among Catholic workers, its movement beyond collective bargaining and thus its distinctive status among North American unions.
251 pages
Paperback ISBN: 0-919618-15-4 $7.95
Hardcover ISBN: 0-919618-14-6 $18.95

WORKING IN CANADA
edited by Walter Johnson
2nd revised edition

These highly original, revealing accounts are based on interviews or written by workers themselves. They allow them to express their thoughts directly: what they do, what they feel about it, what kind of changes they want, and what they think should be done. Johnson is a worker who wrote a definitive study of strikes in Canada, *The Trade Unions and the State;* in this book he provides a preface, introduction and concluding essay, all of which have been brought up to date for this new edition.

Johnson's book is dominated by the most articulate and aware workers who are involved, self-sacrificing and critical.
Books in Canada
160 pages
Paperback ISBN: 0-920057-13-6 $12.95
Hardcover ISBN: 0-920057-14-4 $29.95

THE COMING OF WORLD WAR THREE
VOL.1
From Protest to Resistance/The International War System
by Dimitrios Roussopoulos

This profound and timely work analyses the various forces which bring us ever closer to nuclear annihilation. It also takes the reader on a tour of the numerous anti-nuclear and disarmament organisations worldwide, and identifies a myriad of political issues contributing to international tension. The author offers sympathetic yet critical analysis of the movement, country by country, in a last-ditch attempt to make both activists and the public see the issues clearly and take action to prevent a third world war.

Offers a detailed description of the activities of the anti-nuclear campaign of the 1980s...provides an information resource not readily available elsewhere.
Canadian Book Review Annual

299 pages
Paperback ISBN: 0-920057-02-0 $14.95
Hardcover ISBN: 0-920057-03-9 $29.95

THE COMING OF WORLD WAR THREE
VOL. 2
A New Agenda: From Resistance to Social Change
by Dimitrios I. Roussopoulos

Volume 2 examines the mounting of the new anti-war movement, observing that peace groups have departed significantly from those of the 1960s and that although these constitute a new social movement, they cannot counteract the thrust of the international war system. The author argues for a synthesis of experience and consciousness and for solidarity with other movements in order to produce fundamental social change.

Indispensable reading for all peace activists and thoughtful people generally who are concerned with the future of our planet and our freedom.
Murray Bookchin

Roussopoulos faces a fear that is rapidly becoming in all our minds a certainty we dare not admit—the coming of World War III. The only way to defuse the certainty is by mass popular action on a larger scale than ever before so that at least we can add an "unless" to the phrase "the war will happen."
George Woodcock

200 pages
Paperback ISBN: 0-920057-85-3 $14.95
Hardcover ISBN: 0-920057-83-7 $29.95

BLACK ROSE BOOKS
has published the following books of related interests

Peter Kropotkin, Memoirs of a Revolutionist, introduction by George Woodcock
Peter Kropotkin, Mutual Aid, introduction by George Woodcock
Peter Kropotkin, The Great French Revolution, introduction by George Woodcock
Peter Kropotkin, The Conquest of Bread, introduction by George Woodcock
        other books by Peter Kropotkin are forthcoming in this series
Marie Fleming, The Geography of Freedom: The Odyssey of Elisée Reclus,
        introduction by George Woodcock
William R. McKercher, Freedom and Authority
Noam Chomksy, Language and Politics, edited by C.P. Otero
Noam Chomsky, Radical Priorities, edited by C.P. Otero
George Woodcock, Pierre-Joseph Proudhon, a biography
Murray Bookchin, Remaking Society
Murray Bookchin, Toward an Ecological Society
Murray Bookchin, Post-Scarcity Anarchism
Murray Bookchin, The Limits of the City
Murray Bookchin, The Modern Crisis
Edith Thomas, Louise Michel, a biography
Walter Johnson, Trade Unions and the State
John Clark, The Anarchist Moment: Reflections on Culture, Nature and Power
Sam Dolgoff, Bakunin on Anarchism
Sam Dolgoff, The Anarchist Collectives
Sam Dolgoff, The Cuban Revolution: A critical perspective
Thom Holterman, Law and Anarchism
Stephen Schecter, The Politics of Urban Liberation
Etienne de la Boétie, The Politics of Obedience
Abel Paz, Durruti, the people armed
Juan Gomez Casas, Anarchist Organisation, the history of the F.A.I.
Voline, The Unknown Revolution
Dimitrios Roussopoulos, The Anarchist Papers
Dimitrios Roussopoulos, The Anarchist Papers 2

send for a complete catalogue of books
mailed out free
BLACK ROSE BOOKS
3981 boul. St-Laurent #444
Montréal, Québec H2W 1Y5 Canada

**Printed by the workers of
Ateliers Graphiques Marc Veilleux Inc.
Cap-Saint-Ignace, Québec
for
Black Rose Books Ltd.**